LIFE
REALITIES

LIFE
REALITIES

ANNETTE WHITAKER-MOSS

Life Realities
Genre: Christian Writing, Self-help, and Relationships

Copyright © 2024 by Annette Whitaker-Moss

Disclaimer:

All contents available in this book are for educational and self-help purposes only and do not constitute professional advice or counseling. The author and publisher have made efforts to ensure the accuracy and reliability of the information but make no warranties, express or implied, regarding its completeness or applicability.

Special Thanks:

Book Cover Design – Rose Bud Imaginations
FirstEditing.com – Lee Ann

ISBN   978-0-9897657-3-2

PRINTED IN THE UNITED STATES OF AMERICA

Words of Wisdom

Proverbs 16:3

Commit to the LORD whatever you do, and your plans will succeed.

Proverbs 16:9

In his heart a man plans his course, but the LORD determines his steps.

To My Daughter

Raenetra Bostic

You inspire me daily with your strength, resilience, support, love, and kindness. May you always face life's realities with courage and an open heart, knowing that you have the power to shape your own story. Keep dreaming, keep striving, and never lose sight of the incredible person you are. You are truly remarkable!

Love Always, Mom

Rose Bud

Imaginations

The promise of new beginnings

TABLE OF CONTENTS

A Message from the Author xi

Introduction 1

The Journey 4
  Things I've Learned 4
    A Balanced Life.. 4
    Don't Conform to the World 4
    Wisdom... 5
    Change in Life is About Growth...................................... 7

Past, Present, and Future..8
  What is in your life's blueprint?.. 8

Thorns of Life 11
  Situations 11

Love Notes 23

Reflections on Marriage...24

The Subconscious Mind 27
  Working behind the Scenes... 27

Moving Forward 32
  Owning Your Choices 32

About This Thing Called Love 37
  Where Are the Sacrifices? 37

My Everything 43
  But He Doesn't Want to Be My Everything 43

It's the Little Things 48
  That Hurt... 48

Intuition Is a Gift 53
  Why Ignore It? 53

Creating Lasting Memories 60
  Why Would You Not? 60

The Look on His Face Said I Love You 65
  But He Showed Only Politeness....................................... 65

Learn From My Mistakes 72
  Prenuptial Agreement 72

Life Realities...76

Shattered Emotions 76
    The Meltdown 77
    Meaningful Relationships 80
    Abuse 84
    Absentee Father 88
    Siblings 95
    Friendships 97
    Losing a Loved One 100
    Illness 102
    Professional 107
    Homelessness 109

Conclusion **114**
Comprehending the Experiences 114

Adventures – Enjoying the Next Chapter **116**
Setting Goals and Achieving Them 116
    Cancun, Mexico 118
    Copper Mountain, Colorado 119
    Cozumel, Mexico 121
    Carnival Cruise 122
    Las Vegas, Nevada 124
    Antigua and Barbuda 125
    Jamaica 128
    Carnival Cruise – Western Caribbean 130
    Honolulu, Hawaii 131
    Kauai, Hawaii 132
    Maui, Hawaii 134
    Oahu, Hawaii 136
    Orlando, Florida 139
    San Diego, California 140
    Dominican Republic 142
    Cape Cod, Massachusetts 145
    Antigua and Barbuda, Again 150
    Boulder City, NV – Hoover Dam 152

Special Thanks to My Readers **155**

A MESSAGE FROM THE AUTHOR

Overcoming emotional setbacks demands being open and honest with ourselves and others. Let's embrace the passion to tackle our struggles head-on through couples, individual, and group sessions, where we will find the support and understanding we need. By doing so, we achieve breakthroughs that allow us to enjoy life as it should be, feeling thankful and less alone. Remember, in overcoming, we will find strength and comfort.

As we embark on *Life Realities*, let's remember that God guides our steps, giving us the strength to become overcomers, and we are never alone in this journey!

INTRODUCTION

Have you ever faced something that altered your perception of life, like loneliness, divorce, depression, abuse, loss of a loved one, sudden illness, or perhaps homelessness? Despite our efforts to avoid such experiences, certain circumstances are inevitable. If you have not encountered these challenges, continue living; eventually, you will. As we examine the stories of *Life Realities*, the thorns symbolize the struggles and heartbreaks in our lives—shattered emotions. The pain from these thorns hurts, but eventually, things get better.

In the healing journey, we actively gather lessons from our past experiences, pushing ourselves forward to initiate new events for our future. Like a flower blooming, this transformation represents emotions that flourish and remain vibrant, untouched by negativity. By applying the lessons learned from the past, we can embrace and admire our future, similar to how we appreciate blooming roses. We understand that the blooming process commences when we remove the thorns.

Reflecting on life's undiscerning challenges, I recall how bottling up my emotions affected me when I was younger. Unfortunately, life's realities do not discriminate based on age; regrettably, the consequences are real. I wasn't always innocent, so before I share this story, let me clarify: No offense to my siblings. That's just how things were in those days.

As the oldest of five, I often wished and prayed to be an only child because I felt the burden of responsibility in protecting and setting good examples for my siblings while also longing for more attention. Though some may see it as selfishness, it was a genuine need for attention.

In my family, there were four girls and one boy. This distinction stood out significantly because, if God had granted my prayer, I imagined the girls, three besides myself, would be the first to disappear. At the age of 15, death didn't register as finality to me; I envisioned them simply vanishing, as if by magic. Where would they go? I had no answer; my young mind hadn't anticipated that far. I assumed they would return whenever I wished for it. However, reality did not unfold that way.

I received a summer scholarship to attend Rice University, the top university in Texas. On the first day of class, as I proudly strolled the grounds of Rice University, my little brother lost his life when the diesel truck my father was driving collided with another diesel truck parked on the side of the road. He was 12 years old. Can you imagine the guilt I carried for a long time, believing that God had begun to answer my prayer? All I could think was, *God, that's not what I meant. Bring him back, please bring him back! God, please don't let my sisters disappear too!*

My family did not know of this; they are learning about it for the first time now. My mother was also going through a difficult period. If nothing else, I wanted to support her, mainly because "I believed" it was my fault for uttering such a silly prayer.

I lost interest in attending college for an extended period. However, deep down, a genuine desire to go to college persisted, and for that, I am grateful.

A few years later, I had the opportunity to speak with one of my favorite teachers, and she guided me in processing my thoughts in a healthy way, allowing me to move forward.

This book is about the realities of life, sharing experiences, and conquering struggles, heartbreaks, shattered emotions, and the joys of life like a rising sun, the universal symbol of hope. It is a dialogue on overcoming realities and how others conquered them, empowering you to do the same.

My thorn as a young kid serves as just one example. I aim to examine some of the feelings, thoughts, adverse reactions, positive reactions, and resolutions as we probe into the minds of those who have boldly granted me the opportunity to openly discuss their situations of life realities: loneliness, divorce, depression, abuse, loss of a loved one, a sudden illness, homelessness, heartbreak, and the joys of life.

THE JOURNEY

Things I've Learned

A Balanced Life

The Lord is good to those whose hope is in him, to the one who seeks him. It is good to wait quietly for the salvation of the Lord.

(Lam. 3:25-26)

Don't Conform to the World

"Do not conform to the pattern of this world, but be transformed by the renewing of your mind. Then you will be able to 'test' and approve what God's will is—his good, pleasing, and perfect will"
(Rom. 12:1–2).

- Memory replays the past. God does not want me to live in the past.
- I must prepare to receive good things in the future.
- Don't give up or quit. Instead, I must change my focus.

- My choices should always point in the direction of an overcomer.
- Impatience can be costly, and may lead to my biggest mistakes. I must be still during those moments and wait for God's guidance. As a wise man once told me, patience is the weapon that forces deception to reveal itself. Time is not my enemy, but my friend. I must learn to plan and wait for my destiny to unfold.

Wisdom

"If any of you lacks wisdom, you should ask God, who gives generously to all without finding fault, and it will be given to you. But when you ask, you must believe and not doubt because the one who doubts is like a wave of the sea, blown and tossed by the wind. That person should not expect to receive anything from the Lord" (Jas. 1:5-7).

- I control my present circumstances. If things are wrong, I have allowed them to be so. I will not seek remedies as long as I can endure the problems.
- I will only change once I decide that I will not tolerate it.
- I cannot complain about my circumstances if I allow my circumstances to exist.
- I can't help anyone when I am depressed, confused, upset, or spiritually lost. I must take a stand and re-focus to reach my

true destiny. God will always be with me when pursuing something within his will.

- I must examine myself and my situation to determine what I want to do with my life. It is the first step in making my future whatever I want.

- If I am unwilling to confront my problems, I will be unable to solve them.

- When mistakes are made, confessing them to God and others and asking for forgiveness allows me to move forward.

- Experiencing pain in life is a warning that something is wrong. It lets me know it's time for a fix or a change.

- A breakup or ending often signals the beginning of a whole new life.

- Instead of worrying about everything, pray about it. Let God know what is needed, then thank him for all he is doing, will do, and has done.

- I must believe in myself and others, but ultimately, I must believe in God. I must have faith in God and his word. It is the most crucial element in life. Without faith, it is impossible to please God.

Change in Life is About Growth

- Change is inevitable. It comes whether I want it or not. I must stay at a different level. If I don't like something, I should change it. But if I can't change it, I should change my thoughts.

- When the time comes to change, I must have the courage to take the next step.

- Tomorrow is always happening; therefore, I should always look toward building my future. That means staying focused and recognizing that an idle mind is a mind without a focus.

- Learning to manage my thoughts helps me to win in my mind. If I lose in my mind, I will fail.

- The environment is vital. A suitable climate produces growth that keeps me excited and stimulated.

- When I live in God's presence, I live in a loving environment.

- The meaning of wisdom is to understand what is true, correct, and lasting. I will make good decisions because wisdom will lead me in the right direction toward a loving environment, discernment, and success.

- I permit myself to grieve the ending of a relationship so I can encourage myself to start a new beginning.

- Always remember that my mistakes are not more potent than the purpose God has for me. Therefore, I should make decisions that will benefit my future.

PAST, PRESENT, AND FUTURE
What is in your life's blueprint?

In 1967, Dr. Martin Luther King Jr. delivered a speech to the Barratt Junior High School students. Fifty-plus years later, his powerful words resonate and remain vivid in our society today. He told the students, "This is a most important and crucial period in your lives. What you do now and decide at this age may well determine which way your life shall go." He further explained, "The question is whether you have a proper, a solid, and a sound blueprint" (Kris, 2017). So, what does this imply for our past, present, and future? Well, Dr. Martin Luther King Jr. proposed the following:

1. "A deep belief in your own dignity, your worth, and your own somebodiness." The word *somebodiness* means a sense of being somebody worthwhile, someone who is valued and respected. Dr. Martin Luther King Jr. emphasized, "Don't allow anybody to make you feel that you are nobody. Always feel that you count. Always feel that you have worth, and always feel that your life has ultimate significance" (Kris, 2017).

- We should absolutely embrace this mindset, but some individuals only develop it once they have experienced specific challenges and heartbreaks of life's realities. Regardless of the circumstances, acquiring this mindset at some point in our lives is better than never obtaining it at all.

2. "In your life's blueprint you must have as a basic principle the determination to achieve excellence in varies fields of your endeavor. You're going to be deciding as the days and the years unfold what you will do in life, what your life's work will be. And, once you discover what it will be, set out to do it, and to do it well" (Kris, 2017).

   - This fundamental principle emphasizes achieving excellence through your own efforts. It doesn't focus on excelling in someone else's endeavors. Dr. Martin Luther King Jr. advocated, "Decide what you will do in life, what your life's work will be, and excel at it." Lead your own path to success rather than following others.

   - "And finally, in your life's blueprint there must be a commitment to the external principles of beauty, love, and justice. Don't allow anybody to pull you so low as to make you hate them. Don't let anybody cause you to lose your self-respect to the point that you do not struggle for justice" (Kris, 2017).

Dr. Martin Luther King Jr.'s recommendations resonate deeply with me as I convey the message of *Life's Realities*. There is no simple answer to the question, what should I do? By sharing these experiences, I hope to inspire someone with an open heart, a discerning mind, and the determination and passion to become a conqueror. These concepts are vital to understanding the life we've experienced (the past), the life we are currently living (the present), and the life as we move forward (the future).

THORNS OF LIFE
Situations

In the hallowed halls of many homes, the age-old saying echoes, "What happens in this house stays in this house." But why, one might ponder, does such a statement exist if all is well within these walls?

It's similar to the old saying about Las Vegas, the Sin City: "What happens in Vegas stays in Vegas." It implies that within these boundaries, one can waste one's life savings, creating an experience that could be nothing short of extraordinary. The question lingers: Who genuinely reaps the most benefit from this declaration—the family's respected reputation, the transgressor, or the blameless?

Life Realities doesn't focus on exposing hidden truths; instead, it probes into the healing process from these secrets to break free from the thoughts that trap us in our current circumstances. It's about moving forward, embracing, and celebrating life's moments, just like the blossoming of roses.

Harboring secrets might shield the family name or protect the wrongdoer. But it offers no solace to innocent or distressed people like you, me, or anyone facing life's challenges and striving for personal growth. We must recognize that life unfolds in countless ways, influencing the choices that mold our destinies for better or worse. Therefore, we must eliminate these secrets because we are the architects of our destinies, channeling our energies toward living our most fulfilling lives. Consider, for example, the children who find themselves shouldering the weight of their parents' disputes, attributing it to their own actions. It's heartbreaking to witness a child wrestling with thoughts like, *maybe if I excel in school, Mama and Daddy will find harmony,* or, *If I withhold what I witnessed Daddy doing last night when he took me with him to visit his girlfriend, maybe they will rediscover their love and forget about divorce.*

Additionally, consider the teenager who constantly runs away from home, driven by bottled-up emotions. Ineffective communication between the parents and the teenager leaves issues unresolved, escalating into possibly unhealthy circumstances like drugs, sex trafficking, or getting involved with the wrong crowds.

Think, too, of a dysfunctional family where a young woman endures years hearing her father incessantly belittling her mother. Then, in the heat of the moment, those exact demeaning words are thrown at her: "Your mother is nothing but a whore and a slut… only good for laying on her back, just like you." It is profoundly distressing for a father to utter such derogatory words to his own child.

Consider the elderly individuals who devoted their lives to work and the support of their children. Yet, when they need the same love and consideration, their children calmly declare, "We will find a good nursing home nearby so we can visit you as frequently as possible."

The impact of these words on a parent is unimaginable, causing significant pain, mainly when older adults are powerless to alter their circumstances. Many of us have either seen such stories or witnessed them on TV. Recognizing the distinctiveness of each scenario, we comprehend that some parents require extra care that their children might be unable to provide. Therefore, the statement portrays individuals who unwaveringly decline the notion of looking after their parents in their own homes, driven by self-centered motives.

Think about individuals who once thrived in comfort and prosperity, seemingly balanced at the pinnacle of success. Among them were those earning six-figure incomes, yet they suddenly plummeted to rock bottom. Whether due to job loss, financial mismanagement, or unforeseen events, these individuals found themselves desperately needing government assistance—a situation they had sworn to avoid. For some, this distressing turn of events led to homelessness and seeking refuge in shelters, while others faced the torment of contemplating suicide.

Consider the parents who strive to shield their children from life's trials and tribulations, only to end up with shattered hearts. They shoulder heavy burdens, often depleting their savings as their children repeatedly get into trouble, associate with the wrong crowd, confront law enforcement, or even face incarceration.

Then, there are situations beyond our control that unfold, such as the challenge of raising children with special needs or the sudden start of an illness or disease. These circumstances bring along pain, mental stress, fatigue, and the looming possibility of death. Individuals who persistently stand by their loved ones in these conditions, providing love and support while dealing with their own mental turmoil, deserve our utmost respect and understanding. What steps do they take once the crisis subsides? The answer lies in the actions they choose to embrace. Ultimately, the quality of our lives is shaped by how we confront the challenges that life throws our way.

Every individual on this earth is bound to encounter some manifestation of life's realities. When we observe people from the outside, we only witness what they choose to disclose. Yet, behind closed doors, a different story may unfold—a tale of love and intimacy. Allow me to share two examples of individuals and their circumstances, plainly illustrating the consequences of not grasping the essence of Dr. Martin Luther King Jr.'s message, which emphasizes, "Always feel that you have worth, and always feel that your life has ultimate significance" (Kris, 2017).

Sometimes, our thoughts may lead us to believe there is no way out. However, even in the aftermath of poor decisions, we possess the power to transform our circumstances by altering our thought processes and responses.

Several Investigation Discovery channels, such as TVOne, Crime News, Snapped, Oxygen, and True Crime, broadcast the stories of two girls I like to discuss due to the nature of their crimes. It's hard to ignore the potential divergence in these girls' lives had they known and comprehended their own self-worth. The significance of self-worth cannot be overstated. It could have been transformative if these girls had understood Dr. King's fundamental life truths and embraced their characteristic worthiness.

In the story of Falicia Blakely, a sixteen-year-old teenager in Atlanta, Georgia, a tragic documentary unfolds as one of the most heart-wrenching tales, in my opinion. Her choices, spanning three years, wreaked havoc on her past, present, and future. As an exotic dancer, she finds love in all the wrong places, leading to pregnancy, involvement in stripping, prostitution, robbery, contracting diseases, and ultimately, facing imprisonment. She goes on a murderous rampage, allegedly forced because she met a man who sold her an enormous pipe dream: love, time, playing the role of her baby's father, gifts—coats and cars.

Eventually, he becomes her pimp, degrading her until she becomes conditioned to accept it, something she did not expect because she thought she was special. *Typical thinking of girls in this situation*. It's better known as brainwashing, a process that involves manipulating someone's thoughts and beliefs through intensive programming, propaganda, and psychological pressure. Understanding this process is crucial, as it reveals the manipulator's significant role in systematically breaking down the individual's sense of self, replacing their original ideas with new, imposed beliefs.

This process often includes isolating the person from outside influences, using the powerful tool of repetitive messaging, and inducing stress or fear to weaken resistance. As a result, the brainwashed individual adopts the desired mindset and behaviors of the manipulator, which is precisely why Falicia Blakely believed in the pipe dream.

Unfortunately, she pleads guilty to robbing and murdering three men, a choice that leads to three consecutive life terms without the possibility of parole. Her love, once a guiding light, now blinds her to the consequences. She bravely takes full responsibility for the murders, keeping his name out of it to preserve his affection. Fear and entrapment tighten their hold on her, leaving no doubt that she is ready to take his place in prison. Manipulated and burdened with overwhelming psychological challenges, she now confronts the consequences on her own.

The most distressing aspect of this entire ordeal is that Falicia, her mother, her child, and the families of those who were murdered or harmed are now left heartbroken. Yet, there is a glimmer of hope for redemption in their future. They must all find a way to cope with the extreme repercussions of Falicia's decisions. Is she destined to be lost forever? Can any good arise from this situation? It depends on the perspective one takes, which becomes the crucial factor.

From Falicia's mother's perspective, she passionately believes she has reclaimed her daughter from the streets, liberating her from the life that ultimately led to her incarceration. The fact that Falicia is alive allows her mother to visit her as much as possible. However, the ultimate answers to the situation lie between Falicia and God, which invites deep scrutiny.

Though legally, life beyond the prison walls may remain unreachable for her, her choices from this point forward will chart the actual course of her existence. At this point, we must remember that we are exploring discussions about eternity.

The realities of life carry significant weight in people's lives. Many share the sentiment that the initial stages of relationships typically bring joy. However, all too often, these relationships end in heartbreak.

When we consider stories like those of Falicia Blakely, it raises the question: Is love genuinely blind? Does it blind individuals to the extent that they cannot acknowledge their own discontentment? If so, it emphasizes the need for self-reflection in relationships. The value of peace of mind cannot be overstated, as it surpasses the turmoil of fretting over someone else's problems. Fading into the background and losing oneself while not understanding one's self-worth is a heavy price.

Despite their differences, these stories share striking similarities. The characters in these stories face the same sequence: brainwashing that leads to a loss of personal freedom and a sense of imprisonment due to the consequences of their actions.

As you read, you will surely come to the same conclusion: they sacrificed their identities for seemingly irrational reasons, revealing the final lack of self-worth. Although Falicia and Keshia made their choices with serious thought and consideration, while we may not understand their intense struggle and vulnerability, we experience profound sympathy and compassion for their predicament.

Nineteen-year-old Keshia Renee Smith finds herself becoming the target of a drug dealer during her time at a community college in San Bernardino, California. In the college environment, she crosses paths with a charming student with an outgoing personality, yet this young man is not interested in pursuing an education. His true goal is to expand his drug business, utilizing the college campus as a tactical location.

Initially, he invests a substantial amount of time in displaying affection, professing his love, and providing protection, effectively causing Keshia to develop strong feelings for him, the same tactics used on Falicia Blakely.

Now, ladies, we know how this scenario can unfold. Due to this awareness, we must not disregard the possibility that a man may only be pretending to achieve his true objectives with affection. Therefore, we should always be cautious and mindful of our intuition, staying informed and prepared for any potential manipulation. The old saying goes: "If it sounds too good to be true, it probably is." In which case, it was for Keshia. Her story is troubling because she initially devotes herself to pursuing her college interests until the unexpected love, affection, and attention alter her course.

According to the TVOne *For My Man* documentary, Keshia has faced numerous hardships in life, resulting in low self-esteem. In the process, she loses sight of her own worth and convinces herself she is nothing without this man. In an attempt to impress him, she engages in illegal activities and ends up getting apprehended for theft. The willingness to commit such an act without force highlights her vulnerability to this man's affection.

The judge issues her a probation sentence and outlines that the final sentencing will occur in three months, emphasizing the need to maintain a clean record. However, Keshia perceives the criminal function as a rite of passage, a means to enter her man's criminal world of burglarizing houses and reselling stolen items to fund their drug trade.

The plan succeeds, solidifying their partnership in crime. As a result of Keshia's choices, they proceed to rob the home of another drug dealer, a man residing with his parents and his ninety-year-old grandmother. Unfortunately, Keshia and her partner initiated the robbery while the grandmother was alone in the house. Startled, she pleads with them not to harm her, but they turn a deaf ear to her pleas. Keshia's partner instructs her to tie up the grandmother and cover her head with a pillowcase. He then strikes the ninety-year-old grandmother on the head, presumably to silence her. They proceed to beat and smother her to death.

The sudden eruption of violence shocks Keshia, as it is different from her previous actions. While she is willing to engage in theft, the prospect of causing harm or taking a life is beyond her intentions. At that moment, she realizes she is still on probation and in trouble.

The next day, news arrives of the passing of the ninety-year-old grandmother. Filled with fear and uncertainty, Keshia plans her next steps. Initially, she attempts to continue as if nothing has happened, and, for the moment, she manages to evade detection. At this stage, there is insufficient evidence to convict either Keshia or her partner for the murder.

Three weeks later, the court hands down a four-year sentence to Keshia for violating her probation. Seeking a more lenient punishment, she receives an offer for a plea deal. Despite this opportunity, she adamantly refuses to disclose any information to the authorities regarding her partner's involvement in robberies or the murder of the elderly grandmother.

In contrast, authorities sentenced her partner to fifteen days for possession of the stolen property. Following his release on bail, he moves forward, eventually marrying and starting a family. Due to insufficient evidence to charge the two individuals with the murder of the ninety-year-old grandmother, the case is closed.

Keshia and her man think they are home free, assuming that serving their sentences will end their ordeal. However, to their astonishment, someone reopens the case eight years later. Even then, Keshia remains tight-lipped about her partner's involvement, while he denies ever being inside the house and takes no responsibility for the robberies or the murder. This time, however, there is sufficient evidence to file charges against both Keshia and her partner for the murder. Consequently, they are both currently serving life sentences in prison without the possibility of parole.

Keshia surrenders a life overflowing with opportunities for a man who provides her with nothing in return. Like Falicia, she undergoes heartbreak due to her decisions and now suffers from the repercussions of those choices.

Will life's realities, like blooming roses, intertwine with her existence? The same question lingered with Falicia, with the ultimate answer being between her and God. Likewise, legally, she may only dwell within the prison walls. Her choices from this point onward will mold her life during her imprisonment and for all eternity.

Dr. Martin Luther King Jr's speech certainly holds relevance for the narratives of Falicia Blakely and Keshia Renee Smith: "For what you do now and decide now, at this age, may well determine which way your life shall go" (Kris, 2017).

Indeed, this wisdom applies to each of our lives today!

LOVE NOTES

- Decide to overcome right now!
- Recognize the signs of heartbreak before it occurs.
- Choose not to be lonely; it's a decision, not a determination.
- You can overcome depression, renew your thinking, and make that choice.
- Don't tolerate physical or mental abuse; it's your decision, your choice!

REFLECTIONS ON MARRIAGE

Marriage is a testament to love, resilience, and partnership, where two individuals choose to navigate life's challenges together. The union demands unwavering commitment, honest communication, and a deep understanding of one another. When couples embrace these principles, they create a foundation strong enough to weather any storm.

In marriage, each partner should become both a mirror and a support, reflecting strengths and vulnerabilities while offering comfort and encouragement. Where growth and compromise intertwine, the true essence of marriage should reveal a bond that evolves and strengthens over time, turning two lives into one shared journey.

Just as marriage thrives on mutual support and understanding, the passion we bring into the marriage is a driving force that deepens our connection and enriches our shared journey. Our passion ignites creativity, fuels perseverance, and propels us toward meaningful achievements. Embracing and pursuing our passions together not only enhances our own experiences but also has the power to inspire and positively impact those around us. For this reason, I am eager to express the profound importance of passion in our marriages, as it is a critical factor in achieving significant milestones.

After experiencing two failed marriages, I have developed a craving for helping married couples understand their situation by amplifying the voices of their loved ones, which is especially important for closed-minded couples. My journey has taught me that offering a different perspective from a unique vantage point can aid spouses unwilling to consider alternative ideas or opinions. Understanding your partner's perspective is crucial, and empowers you to embrace the admirable challenge of navigating marriage.

Love is beautiful when couples find themselves happily married because the wife meets her husband's needs, and the husband meets his wife's needs. When we take the focus off ourselves, needs are no longer selfish acts. Instead, the spouses meet each other's needs, working together as a team. As the two become one, they eliminate division and emphasize the strength of unity in marriage, creating a deep sense of connection and security for one another.

Consider the following: we can function with just one eye, one ear, one arm, one leg, or one foot, but when joined together, we are more robust and productive. The concept is easier to understand when considering how our limbs operate, meeting the intended purpose. This analogy extends to married couples who, when they join together as one, become part of a larger whole, complete, more vital, fulfilled, and happy, while fostering a deep sense of unity and togetherness.

Recognizing your relationship's commitment level is mandatory, especially before marriage. This book's examples of conversations and stories play a crucial role in guiding you through this recognition, providing reassurance and clarity. Gaining clarity on your commitment better equips you to manage the inevitable conflicts that arise once the initial excitement fades. The goal is to avoid or resolve them in a way that positively impacts your future together.

If you're already married and facing challenges, it's important to remember the initial passion and commitment you once had. It's not always easy, but perseverance and creativity are vital to keeping the fire burning in your relationship. Remember, a meaningful and enjoyable marriage is worth the effort, so thoughtful consideration is crucial.

THE SUBCONSCIOUS MIND

Working behind the Scenes

As I neared my bedroom, a sudden, unexpected movement seized my attention—a dark shadow rushing swiftly through my peripheral vision, distracting my subconscious mind while shaping my reality. Alone in the house, I had double-checked everything before setting the alarm. Yet, there I stood, frozen but determined to confirm what I had just witnessed.

As I stepped into the bedroom, I instinctively lowered the TV volume, my senses on high alert for unusual sounds. Convinced of the silence, I switched off the lights, settled into bed, and pulled the covers over my head, ready for a peaceful night's sleep.

But my mind, refusing to rest, conjured up vivid images of a figure looming over me and breathing heavily. With a growing sense of unease, I cautiously peeked from beneath the covers, only to find an empty room.

Suddenly, an irrational urge prompted me to look under the bed— a thought unjustified given the limited space beneath the bed, hardly enough for a broom, let alone a person. I was left with a sense of confusion, unable to understand the source of my fear.

My subconscious mind had convinced me that a stalker was inside my home, a notion that seemed ridiculous. I cautioned myself, thinking, *Girl, stop this! Just stop this nonsense!* After a mental reset, I took charge, allowing my mind to rest. With a newfound clarity, I was able to overcome the fear and enjoy a restful night.

I am amazed at how our subconscious processes vast amounts of information without conscious awareness, storing memories, habits, and automatic responses, some deceiving and some driving us toward goals and desires imprinted deep within our psyche.

Has your subconscious mind ever deceived you, especially during challenging relationships? Think about how easily it can be pushed into overdrive. A simple song can have a significant influence. Picture this: you enjoy the beat, the instruments, the melody, and perhaps the lyrics. Then, in a sudden shift, you find yourself fixating on the words, visualizing their meaning, and pondering how they relate to your own experiences.

I don't know about you, but one song gets me every time. Do you recall the singer La Porsha Renae, who displayed her talent on the *American Idol* show in 2015? Her first album, *Already Already*, includes the song "Good Woman" (Renae, 2016), where the chorus lyrics imply that even good women go bad when treated a certain way.

Now, concentrate on the first two lines emphasizing that this man has a good woman, as if you play the song daily, repeating it often as we do if we genuinely enjoy the music. Can you sense the bitterness building up inside? I certainly can. If I play this song every day while driving home from work, my husband's face will be the last face I want to see when I open that door. And heaven forbid I develop an interest in another man!

Regardless of what I think, my subconscious will rationalize it with the last two lines: "Cuz, I'm a real good, good, good, good, woman (woman). But even good women go bad when they go through what you put me through" (Renae, 2016).

Every word in the song underscores the crucial role of a husband—to be loving, caring, intimate, provider, and protector. However, maintaining this attitude after continuously listening to the song can prevent reconciliation, even if the man is willing to reconsider and make amends.

Intimacy, the most profound physical and emotional connection between a man and a woman, is crucial for a relationship to thrive. However, a woman's ability to sustain a flourishing relationship can be severely hindered if she conceals emotional chaos. This disorder can manifest in various ways, such as withdrawal, increased arguments, or a lack of interest in intimacy. The impact of this emotional chaos on her ability to sustain a relationship is significant, as her subconscious nurtures insecurities, frustrations, and even thoughts of revenge, like finding another man. She may appear composed to external observers, but deep within her heart, where it truly matters, the bruises multiply and the bitterness escalates.

A man's subconscious is a complex entity that significantly influences his emotions, often in ways he may not fully realize. The male psyche holds a fascinating aspect that we rarely explore. I believe men typically don't focus on lyrics like women, so it may not be as direct as a song. However, it can still generate feelings of insecurity, frustration, and unfaithfulness, or even push him towards a drastic step like ending the relationship.

Understanding this influence not only leads to greater self-awareness and enlightenment but also empowers him, giving him a sense of control and confidence to set things right, or convince him there's no desire to mend things. The subconscious also has the potential to promote change, inspire, and motivate.

I find matters of the heart intriguing, particularly the importance of examining men's and women's experiences. Their emotions, responses, and decisions often vary, despite facing similar heartbreak. Did you know that a man or a woman can reside in the same house as a significant other and still feel lost and lonely, merely navigating through life's motions without any satisfaction? Some of them maintain their appearance, while others seem to let themselves go. Could those who keep their appearance be mindful of a life beyond their current situation, striving to overcome it?

On the other hand, for those who don't, perhaps it's because they are content or even struggling with depression, leading them to ponder, "Why bother?" This examination is not just intriguing, but also important in understanding the human experience.

Indeed, I'm not employing the same example for a man. I seek insight from a man's perspective to analyze. However, I can assert, men and women differ, and as a result, they think differently, potentially having fluctuating viewpoints on matters of the heart.

The events in a person's life, whether a man or a woman, don't exclusively determine the course of their future. It's their active management of these events that shape the path of what their lives will become. This understanding empowers us to take control of our lives. Remember, silence can heal or destroy because "the tongue has the power of life and death" (Prov. 18:21). Therefore, one must exercise caution regarding thoughts and ideas in their subconscious, as they may inadvertently lead them down unintended paths.

MOVING FORWARD
Owning Your Choices

H ave you ever broken a promise to God by doing exactly what you vowed not to do? I must confess I have, and I'm not proud of it. Despite having every intention of keeping my promise, I completely forgot about it when the time came.

Fortunately, this is no surprise to God. He knows full well that we will break our promises. *Thank you, Lord, for granting me new mercy and grace daily. I am deeply grateful!*

After reading this story, I'm sure many of you will form your own opinions. Some of you might have taken more significant actions than I did. But before you draw your conclusion, remember that the story isn't about him or them. It's about me taking responsibility for the choices I made. It wasn't enough to just feel guilty; I had to take ownership of my mistake to find redemption. I encourage you to consider your own actions and take ownership of your mistakes.

The events began when my husband and I invited his best friend and his family for dinner. As his wife and I prepared the food, the men's voices escalated in the other room, sounding more like an argument than a casual conversation. Despite the potential stress, I stayed calm and focused on entertaining his wife and kids while we prepared dinner.

His wife was well aware of the situation and contributed to the problem. The kids occupied themselves, playing and watching TV. They were so quiet that I almost forgot they were there. After a while, she asked me, "Do you know what's going on?"

"No," I replied. "Do you?"

"Yes. Your husband and I slept together," she said. In my mind, I thought, *What the heck? Is she trying to be funny, or is she crazy?* But she wasn't laughing, so I remained calm as she explained what occurred.

"It happened when I borrowed the car last week to take the kids to the doctor," she said.

I was puzzled and frowning, all the while thinking, *What? We're helping her and their kids, and she's sleeping with my husband?*

She continued, "I didn't plan it. It just happened when I returned the car."

What the hell is she saying? Nothing "just happens" like that!

In that instant, I almost exploded with, "BITCH, you're out of your mind!" (Excuse my French, as we used to say when I was younger.) The urge to slap her and knock her backward grew within me and I struggled to control it. Somehow, I managed my anger and considered those two innocent kids sitting in my living room. I did not want them to witness their mom and me fighting, and that thought was the only thing that kept me from losing control.

My mind was racing, entirely out of character. I struggled to keep a composed expression when I asked, "How did your husband find out?"

When she responded, "I told him," I was dumbfounded. *Why would she confess this to him?* A storm of emotions raged through my mind as she added, "In our marriage, we share everything, no matter how difficult it may be. This has always been our way, a way to address our issues, forgive one another if necessary, and move on. So, I told him."

What? Really? You're going to jeopardize my marriage while resolving your problems! I thought, and wanted to express it, but the words refused to leave my lips. I was left speechless, struggling to comprehend the situation. The room was completely silent after that statement. There was nothing left to say until the guys rejoined us.

After the argument, the two men left the room, with anger evident on my husband's friend's face, and the family departed. I expected my husband to acknowledge his wrongdoing and, if nothing else, apologize. Instead, he lay on the sofa in complete silence.

His lack of communication only added to my frustration. But as he made no effort to stop me from leaving, my anger grew, reaching a boiling point. His silence was highly disappointing. I felt not just heartbroken, but utterly alone.

With no specific place to go and a reluctance to turn to my family, I reached out to a guy who lived nearby, whom I had met in the local grocery store a few weeks earlier. I asked if I could come over. He responded, "Sure, I'm having a house party tonight. You're more than welcome to join." I explained that I wasn't in the mood for a party; I just needed a safe place to spend the night. It was a desperate plea for asylum, a moment of vulnerability I rarely allowed myself to show.

He kindly agreed, saying, "That's fine too. You can stay in my room during the party." After entertaining his guests, he asked if I needed to talk, so we did. I found myself in tears and, in my vulnerable state, more than sleep occurred in that room that night. It was a moment of sweet relief, a feeling of sweet revenge that I desperately needed, but the conflicting emotions of guilt and relief were overwhelming.

Thankfully, God, in his benevolence, grants us, his children, the freedom to make our own choices in life, a truly remarkable gift. In any given situation, we have the power to choose a positive or negative attitude, ultimately shaping the course of our lives. The responsibility for the consequences, good or bad choices, rests with us (Deut. 28:1-68).

But when we make the wrong choice, we may need assistance in understanding our circumstances. This understanding is key to transforming our thinking and evolving as more vigorous and better individuals while embracing the journey of forgiving ourselves and others.

I consider guilt a stronghold that hinders our progress. When we forgive others for their wrongdoings, we must remember to forgive ourselves. This self-forgiveness is not just a step but a leap toward the love, peace, joy, and happiness we desire. (Gal. 5:22-23) It may not always be easy, but it is unquestionably worth the effort and the valuable aftermath it brings.

So, there it is! Your thoughts are your own, but before passing judgment on either side, remember that you don't know what you will do until you walk a mile in someone else's shoes, as the old saying goes.

ABOUT THIS THING CALLED LOVE
Where Are the Sacrifices?

Imagine a cheesy, mouthwatering slice of meat lover's pizza with ground beef, pepperoni, Canadian bacon, mushrooms, olives, and veggies that could have been yours. Instead, you graciously turned away, leaving it for your spouse.

That's exactly how it should be. It's like becoming a superhero, but instead of a cape, you wear the badge of selflessness, proudly proclaiming with a smirk, "I sacrificed my snack for love!" *Who needs superpowers when you've got a heart filled with love and a satisfied stomach full of sacrifice?* It's not about personal gain but the importance and value of showing love.

In a marriage, partners willingly embark on a significant journey, sacrificing their personal needs for the sake of each other. This commitment forges an unspoken oath between husband and wife, a sincere promise that transcends the mere utterance of I love you. The details of this commitment reveal a complexity that goes beyond the simplicity of spoken vows. Remember, the love affair starts before the vows.

- We enjoy and explore shared interests.
- We confide in each other, building a bond.
- We share hopes and fears as we listen, comprehend, and respond appropriately.
- We embrace each other's quirks and flaws, finding joy in the little things.

Before expressing that you love someone, understanding the importance of communication—including listening, comprehension, and knowing how to respond to one another—is crucial. Simply enjoying someone's company during social events, date nights, phone conversations, or even spontaneous sexual encounters does not necessarily indicate being in love with that person. These types of relationships typically operate smoothly in the beginning. In today's society, they can signify various things, such as friendships, friends with benefits, or even manipulation. Listening, comprehending, responding appropriately, and being patient with the individuals we engage with is vital, especially before saying I do.

Patience in communication is a key factor that reassures us that we can truly take the time to understand each other. Yet, despite our best efforts, certain issues can arise that cause problems in marriage.

As you say I do and step into the future, you may encounter communication, intimacy, and financial issues—three common causes of relationship strain. These challenges, often overlooked in the dating phase, can suddenly surface, causing you to question the sustainability of your marriage.

It's important to remember that these are opportunities for growth and learning, not just obstacles. The longevity of your marriage depends on the effort you're willing to invest. Sustaining a marriage requires a significant commitment to give and take, but more importantly, it requires a deep mutual understanding and respect for each other's needs and feelings.

As an ex-wife, I can affirm that the relationship deteriorates if the two individuals cannot communicate and resolve issues effectively. When I articulate my needs and desires to my husband, I expect him to listen, understand, and respond to my requests. Disregarding my needs and desires conveys a lack of respect for my worth. Despite his claims of love, respect, and adoration, his actions carry more weight than his words. It's the tangible evidence of his love and respect that truly matters. I demand this evidence demonstrating my importance through what he says, hears, and feels.

Likewise, he must witness, listen, and sense his significance to me by my behavior. Without such tangible displays, a similar conversation, which appears as empty words, may go as follows:

I asked my husband, "Honey, do you have life insurance with me as the beneficiary?"

He replied, "No, I haven't considered it, given that I was on my own for a long time, and if something were to happen to me, as a veteran's wife, you get a fifteen-hundred-dollar-a-month benefit."

I informed him, "If something happens to me, my insurance policy is valued at three hundred thousand dollars, and would ensure your ability to manage your needs and all other obligations. We should also secure a policy for you, so I have at least the same coverage. Your well-being is just as important as mine." So, I provided him with my agent's contact information and asked him to reach out. He nodded and said OKAY.

Several weeks later, I asked, "What did the agent tell you?"

He replied, "I didn't get in touch with him."

I couldn't help but wonder, why doesn't he consider this important? Tomorrow isn't guaranteed for either of us (Prov. 27:1). If something were to happen to him, could I survive alone? Does he even care?

Three years later, he still lacks a life insurance policy that will take care of my needs after his death. Can you perceive the potential problem we face? I expressed my concern about obtaining his life insurance policy, but he didn't respond or act responsibly. So, how significant am I? I don't feel valued, secure, or loved. I feel neglected. Where is the care, concern, or sacrifice?

Fact #1: Relationships cultivate love when people listen, understand, and respond to one another.

I know men demand respect, and perhaps my husband was thinking, *who does she think I am? She can't instruct me to make an appointment like I'm her child. I'm a grown man. She can't dictate my actions!* But knowing your spouse means recognizing when disrespect occurs. These thoughts suggest more significant issues might be imminent, highlighting difficulties in effective communication. We both must strive for mutual understanding. I also asked him to oversee other important matters, like getting a will in place. It was a simple and manageable plan of action that went unnoticed.

Fact #2: All relationships pivot on communication. What you say and how you perceive it can significantly impact a conversation, potentially leading to misunderstandings or hard feelings.

Another noteworthy experience occurred on our anniversary weekend as we traveled out of town and met with some of my friends. The plan included sightseeing and dinner later in the day, in a setting that was perfect for romance. Considering it was an anniversary celebration, I anticipated we would be intimate sometime after dinner.

However, my friends went to bed for the night, and unfortunately, my husband did the same. I felt deeply disappointed. On our anniversary weekend, he turned his back to me and started snoring. I thought, *What the HELL is this? I didn't sign that marriage license to be celibate! I can count the instances of our intimacy in a year on one hand, which was less than five times. And today, on our anniversary weekend, still NOTHING!*

Where is the sacrifice? I had already endured a year of celibacy. I felt alone, neglected, and undesirable. It was supposed to be a love affair of passion, tenderness, and full of promises, setting the stage for a great future together.

Fact #3: It all depends on how much work you will put into the marriage. Longevity in a marriage demands considerable giving and taking, listening, understanding, and responding to one another's needs.

Our marriage failed from the start because it lacked the commitment needed for longevity.

MY EVERYTHING
But He Doesn't Want to Be My Everything

H e said, "You behave as if you don't care. I'm the last person to know anything about you. You seek advice from everyone else before approaching me. You think you are better than I am."

These words, spoken by the man who once proposed to me, now seem like a cruel joke. He wanted to be my husband, the center of my world. But now, he expected me to treat him like he was everything to me, yet he didn't want to be *my* everything.

How can he be my everything when I ask for intimacy, and he, as my husband, deliberately ignores me? The bed remains empty, and he disregards any discussion on the matter.

In the first year of our marriage, we touched each other intimately three times, but such moments ceased after that, causing me to doubt my femininity. He accused me of acting like I don't care. When did I become so undesirable, and whose actions genuinely communicated a lack of care?

Let's speak candidly and explore different thoughts and emotions. Imagine if someone, in a situation where you needed financial assistance, never offered help, or consistently ignored your requests. The emotional toll of this lack of support can be overwhelming, leading to feelings of isolation and resentment.

Similarly, the consequences of not receiving support from a spouse can be profound, affecting the individual and the relationship as a whole.

When I need support, I turn to someone I trust, and that someone should be my husband, the person I need and value the most. His support is crucial, providing comfort and security to our relationship, where we both play fundamental and equally important roles in each other's lives.

When a man says I do," he protects, provides, and expresses his commitment to his wife. If she voices her need for assistance, he should, within legal boundaries, take whatever steps are necessary to provide the help she requires. Unfortunately, this is not what happened in my marriage.

Instead of receiving support from my husband, I found myself struggling through financial adversity, which disrupted my stability. I now had to ask for help from family and friends, a humbling experience that made me feel like a homeless person holding a sign on the corner.

Consider the weight of your financial burden and the relief you feel when a friend with a disability and minimal income selflessly offers whatever she can, or when an unemployed friend's husband works extra hours to help you out. It's a bittersweet situation. On one hand, you're overwhelmed with gratitude for their selfless acts, which offer a beacon of hope during a dark time. The relief from the financial burden and the indescribable sentiments they bring are truly heartfelt. Their support not only eases the financial strain but also lifts our spirits, reminding us that we're not alone in this struggle.

On the other hand, there's a deep sense of embarrassment when you have to ask for help, especially when your husband is not stepping up. It's heartening to know that even family members like your mother, uncle, and siblings are willing to help. They understand that your husband could secure a temporary part-time job to support his family, especially since he lives in the same household but his actions, or inaction, speak louder than words.

My husband's failure to support me prompted strong reactions, and I must admit, I lost a significant amount of respect for him during that period. Yet, he accused me of behaving as if I didn't care. But whose actions genuinely conveyed a lack of care?

Even as neglect trembled through my heart, hope still lingered within me for a change. I proposed seeking counseling, a decision that required courage and vulnerability to unveil our perspectives and explore the reasons behind our emotions. The possibility of understanding each other better, acting with more significant consideration, overcoming disappointments, and developing effective communication, fueled my optimism. However, the anticipation of his indifferent response was a bitter pill to swallow, filling me with disenchantment.

As expected, he ignored my plea. His lack of concern and motivation to fight for our marriage was apparent. The consequences were evident as our marital bond crumbled, making it obvious that he didn't want this marriage to succeed. It doesn't take a genius to discern this reality.

Reflecting on his accusation, "You think you are better than I am," I questioned why I would choose to marry someone I perceived as beneath me. The logic behind such a decision eludes me as I realized his words were a window into his insecurities.

As a fellow traveler on the marriage journey, I've faced significant challenges with communication, intimacy, and finances. These are not hypothetical issues, but ones I've navigated in my marriage, just like many of you, so you are not alone. Hope is still possible if a couple proactively addresses these concerns early to prevent minor problems from escalating. With the power of love, the fuel of effort, and the desire to succeed, couples manage challenges better because it compels them to work together and navigate through any issues that may arise.

As I conclude, facing these problems head-on promotes a harmonious future where mutual understanding, resilience, and positive efforts strengthen the relationship, the marriage, so he can be my everything, and I can be his!

IT'S THE LITTLE THINGS
That Hurt

Like the sweet early morning kisses planted on my cheek while lying in bed, yet still asleep. Or, just before my eyes have closed, innocent lips whisper, 'good night,' then reach over to touch the other.

(Whitaker-Moss, Another Heart to Another, 2017)

These actions and spoken words originate from the book *Another Heart to Another*. But what happens in relationships when the little things hurt more? The pain is nothing like poking oneself with a needle and shouting ouch, or attempting to remove unwanted hair with scorching wax and later witnessing the evidence of a bad waxing job. It may sting or burn for a moment or two, but it does not compare to the intense, lingering ache of a saddened heart.

Longing for more than a simple peck on the lips from my husband, I was consumed by the desire for a lingering, passionate kiss with the intertwining of tongues. Eventually, I gathered the courage to kindly tell him that I didn't particularly appreciate receiving a daily peck on the lips.

Unfortunately, my attempt to discuss my feelings with him had a more profound impact on our relationship than I had anticipated. What I thought was a harmless conversation turned out to be deeply distressing for him. As a result, the hope for passionate kisses faded, and even the routine peck on the lips became increasingly scarce.

The peck, a small, meaningful gesture, left me yearning for more. I questioned why I couldn't have both – the simple peck *and* the passionate kiss. After all, I was the wife. Was that too much to ask? The little things meant a lot to me, but the small gestures hurt the most.

As for him, I couldn't discern if his feelings were hurt, or why he underwent such a complete change. The lack of clear communication left me confused and hurt, feeling like I had been pranked on a game show, desperately needing clarity, and wondering what just happened?

Little sentimental memories are powerful—and painful when others don't fully grasp their emotional connection. During my childhood, the bonding moments with my grandmother were precious. She lived in a small, wood-frame house with a screened-in front porch, a place of beauty decorated with stunning red roses on each side. Our shared activity of tending the blooms, removing old buds to make way for new ones, was a significant part of our bond. As I reminisce over those days, I miss my grandmother and long for any semblance of what we did together.

When my husband and I purchased our home, I was delighted to find two red rose bushes on each side of the entryway, just like the ones from my childhood. While I adore today's modern landscapes with beautiful knock-out roses, I prefer the rare roses akin to my grandmother's house. Returning home and admiring the roses before I pulled into the garage became my cherished routine. It was a comforting habit that brought back memories of visiting my grandmother, and her voice instructing me on how to tend the roses.

One day, upon my return from work on trash day, I was shocked to find the rose bushes, which had always added a touch of beauty to our entryway, now lying at the end of the driveway, waiting to be picked up by the garbage truck. I was in a state of panic! It was almost impossible to believe that my husband could uproot and discard them, knowing how much they meant to me. He saw the yard as his canvas to tend and beautify according to his vision, and roses at the front door, didn't fit into that picture.

After observing my distress over the fate of the roses, he took swift action before the garbage truck could claim them, rescuing the bushes and replanting them in the backyard the following day. His quick thinking and effort in saving the roses brought me immense relief and gratitude. Despite my desire to have them at the front where I could readily admire them, he stood firm in his decision. Although not entirely pleased with the compromise, I could still find solace in admiring the roses in the backyard.

Those rose bushes were incredibly important to me, despite seeming like a small matter. Something so small shouldn't stir any hatred, but it did because it hurts when someone dismisses your feelings, and you recognize it's the little things that hurt the most.

Once again, knowing how much they meant to me, he discarded the roses in the backyard, cutting the bushes and bagging them up for trash! The question lingered in my mind: *what would it take for this man to understand the significance I placed on those roses?*

I found some relief when I discovered that, despite his actions, some roots materialized underground, enabling one of the rose bushes to regrow. I thought he had finally understood *that the roses should remain, for my sake,* but I was disappointed again when he uprooted the last rose bush, roots and all, showing a complete and frustrating lack of understanding. I was left with a profound sense of disappointment and loss, as if I had lost my grandmother's roses and the memory of precious sentiments.

To this day, I am puzzled by his lack of comprehension. Despite our initial two arguments and my explicit expressions about the importance of the rose bushes, why did he choose to continuously destroy them? The emotional disconnect between us was overpowering. As a woman, I longed for that connection, and found it almost necessary. For me, it was a little thing that inflicted the most hurt.

But let's zero in on the crucial aspect: understanding the root of the problem. It's essential to do this without resorting to blame, whether towards your partner or yourself. This approach allows us to probe into why we react the way we do and, most importantly, how to prevent similar mistakes in relationships moving forward.

I can't grasp why he didn't see the significance of delighting me with the rose bushes. Keeping them wouldn't hurt either of us. But every story has two sides, and this one is mine. His point of view could shed some light on his reactions, but I'm not privileged with such information. I can only attest that the little things hurt the most.

Life's Realities aims to share thoughts and feelings, aiding others in understanding that we all encounter painful experiences and have similar emotions. The goal is to learn from these situations, discover ways to cope, and most importantly, to inspire and motivate others to move forward.

INTUITION IS A GIFT
Why Ignore It?

T he night before my dad's accident, as I prepared to attend my first day at Rice University with the honor of a summer scholarship, I was filled with mixed emotions. Little did I know, this feeling was not just about the next day's excitement, but also a premonition of the tragedy that was about to unfold.

My stomach churned with nervousness like waves against a raging shore, and this mysterious feeling overwhelmed me, intensifying the situation. As the strange feeling emerged, I convinced myself it was nothing to worry about. At that moment, what started as a possible concern quickly became a unique acceptance of my accomplishments and a deep pride in my personal growth and resilience. I had come a long way and was proud to have received such an honor.

As I settled into this newfound confidence, I moved forward with registration. After completing twenty minutes of registration and attending my first scheduled class, the instructor received a message directing me to leave the classroom due to an emergency.

I had barely been in class for five minutes when my two aunts approached me and my mom, who met me at the door, unraveling the mysterious feeling lingering inside me with the news. Exiting the classroom and heading towards the car, I inquired, "What's wrong? Did something happen?"

My aunt responded, "Yes, there's been an accident." My curiosity piqued as I anxiously awaited details about which of my three sisters were in the accident. The anticipation for the news was almost unbearable.

To my surprise, she uttered, "It's your brother." A heavy ache settled in my heart as we silently hurried home to be with the family.

Later, I came to understand that the unique sensation I experienced was my intuition—a divine gift from God, empowering me to perceive things beyond my understanding. It is such a powerful influence that it's hard to fathom why we often overlook it. The Bible, in (Prov. 3:5-6), advises us to move forward wisely, trusting that the Lord guides our steps as we acknowledge and heed our God-given intuition.

In some strange way, I felt prepared for what was about to unfold. Though not armed with the exact facts, there was a real sense that something was on the verge of permanently altering my family's lives. And indeed, it did. If my mind hadn't envisioned the outcome beforehand, my reactions might have been devastating or possibly mentally destructive. Fortunately, I avoided the destruction due to my mental strength and tendency to internalize my feelings.

Reflecting on those instincts, I connected similar experiences to this gift. One instance is my past relationship with an older man who made me feel exceptional—beautiful, loved, and needed. He went to great lengths to keep me happy. However, every month or two, he would deliberately change. His personality shifted, leading to arguments that always resulted in reasons we couldn't spend time together on specific weekends. This relationship, with all its complexities, has played a significant role in shaping my current feelings and perceptions.

Like a private detective, I conducted a stakeout outside his house, meticulously observing his comings and goings. I never witnessed anything odd. Frustration and boredom from the stakeout finally pushed me to confront him about the state of our relationship.

When I asked, he responded, "I don't know what you are talking about."

Tension was in the air as I cut to the chase and asked him, "Are you seeing someone else?"

His firm denial initially lifted a weight off my shoulders, relieving my worries. However, a lingering doubt persisted, casting a shadow over my emotions.

My voice was stern and solid as I issued a clear warning. "If you are, I will find out." This declaration was a testament to my determination to protect myself and our relationship.

He assured me, saying, "There's nothing to catch." Then, he smiled and kissed me on the cheek, but it didn't feel genuine. My intuition cautioned me to be vigilant, to tread carefully.

Determined not to be deceived, I decided to catch him in the act and end his lies. He fooled me once, and probably more times than I care to admit, but this time, I refused to let him make me look like a fool. So, I secretly made a copy of his house key. When my intuition kicked in again, I showed up on his doorstep. As my grandmother used to say, "If you go looking for trouble, you just might find it!" And find it, I did.

I knocked, but there was no answer. Gently turning the key, I opened the door and quietly walked toward the soft music coming from his bedroom. There, I found my man in bed, naked and engaging with some woman. When I called out to him, he quickly jumped up, walked to the restroom, put on his pants, grabbed me by my arm and asked, "What are you doing here?" Meanwhile, the woman grabbed the sheets and covered her head, seemingly embarrassed.

I yelled, "I KNEW YOU WERE LYING! YOU ARE NOT AS SLICK AS YOU THINK YOU ARE!"

All he could say was, "GET OUT OF MY HOUSE! LEAVE," as he guided me toward the door.

At that moment, I learned a valuable life lesson: sometimes, the truth is not worth the trouble it brings. However, I proved my point. As far as I was concerned, the relationship was over. Lesson learned: A smile, a hug, or the appearance of sincerity can fool you if you're not careful.

Once again, my intuition was my guiding light, a reliable force so potent that it's baffling why we often disregard it. We must recognize that reflecting on our behaviors, thoughts, and desires keeps us in tune with our intuition, shaping our decisions.

I recall another instance where following my intuition proved beneficial. Wanting my children to have a good relationship with their father, I let him visit freely. Despite being a good dad, he wasn't always honest with me.

When my car gave me problems, he selflessly offered to have a mechanic friend look at it. He said, "You need your car to get the kids to school and other activities." The same thing happened when I told him I was short of money and needed him to get the kids something to eat. What did he do? His generosity extended to buying groceries for all of us, saying, "You are my kids' mother, and you need to eat too." I thought everything was good and we were doing what was best for our children. Our ability to get along seemed like a promising start towards giving them the best life possible in a divorce situation.

However, I stumbled across a tape recorder hidden inside my car, a discovery that initially left me in disbelief. It shattered my trust and prompted me to search my home for others. I found several recorders throughout the house. It was surprising, but not in a good way, like discovering a prize in every box of the famous snack Cracker Jack. Despite the feeling of someone being in my home several times, everything appeared to be in place, so I initially ignored my intuition. But the evidence soon became unquestionable.

I suspected the kids' dad was the culprit, but I knew I needed solid evidence before making any accusations. So, I put my detective skills to work once more. The plan was to observe him, knowing that the recorders would need to be retrieved at some point. The kitchen, strategically positioned, offered a view of the living area, a bedroom, and the hall entryway. As I was working in the kitchen, I saw him check the sofa and look under the pillows, like a child playing hide-and-seek in the living room. The living room, a key location in this investigation, was where I thought, *I've got him!*

Fortunately, he didn't notice me approaching; otherwise, he might have thought it was too risky to retrieve the recorders since I had a clear view of him from the kitchen. I approached him, raised the recorder, and asked, "Is this what you are looking for?" His reaction was priceless, a perfect mix of shock and surprise. Then, I informed him, "Don't bother looking for others. I found them too."

Like many others, this experience reinforced my understanding that intuition is powerful. So, why ignore it? Instead, I've learned to embrace the God-given gift and be thankful for the times it has gotten me through some challenging situations. It's a gift. Why ignore it?

CREATING LASTING MEMORIES
Why Would You Not?

───────────────

*Why would you not keep me wondering about my
future? So maybe I can forget about my past or bond
with me in lovemaking that's oh so ever sweet, giving
me a vision each night as I lay down to sleep.
Reminding me with a whisper that your love will
forever keep. Reaching and touching my innermost
thoughts while boldly speaking, I got your every need.
You are my one and only, my true love indeed.*

(Whitaker-Moss, Another Heart to Another,
2017)

The words above illustrate a woman speaking from her heart and expressing her desires. In contrast, some men often express desires that emulate their father's treatment and reactions toward their mothers when it depicts love.

For instance, every morning, a son may address his wife as "Sugar" or "Sweetheart," as he witnessed his father saying to his mother. While doing so is perfectly okay and admirable, a man must remember that his wife chose him, not his father. She didn't sign up for a sequel; she picked the original version of her husband so they could create new sayings and lasting memories.

Thinking about it makes sense. No two people are alike; others may respond differently to similar situations. Creating new sayings and lasting memories is not just a possibility but a necessity in relationships, inspiring hope and a sense of purpose. It's a journey of growth and discovery between a husband and wife.

Understanding the importance of commitment in creating enduring memories from a woman's perspective is crucial. A man must commit to these memories, even if his parents have a loving relationship. These memories, whether positive or negative, significantly shape the relationship dynamics. It underscores the importance of commitment in marriage and the potential positive influence of creating lasting, meaningful experiences.

For instance, a husband can create enduring memories by planning surprise date nights, traveling to new places, dining out, or showing appreciation for his wife's efforts with gifts or flowers. These actions can have a positive influence on their relationship dynamic.

Our formative years, whether spent with parents, relatives, or friends, are a rich source of learning about relationship dynamics. Observing these positive and negative actions can profoundly shape our relationship approach. This informative and empowering learning provides us with the tools for personal growth and understanding. But it's crucial to recognize the best individual tactic regarding husband-and-wife dynamics.

I can vividly recall my husband's reflection on his parents' arguments. He recounted, "When my parents argued, my dad would always take a step back, often leaving the house, to prevent things from escalating." His reflection on his parents' arguments is a poignant example of the lasting impact these early experiences can have. It also serves as a cautionary tale, highlighting the potential consequences of misinterpreting these experiences as a blueprint for our relationships, thinking, *It worked for my dad, so it will work for me.*

The uncertainty about how my in-laws resolved their problems lingered in my mind. Did they resume their discussion after things calmed down? I couldn't say for sure. Ignoring me or walking away only intensifies the problem, whether we are calm or not. I am not my husband's mother, and he shouldn't expect me to react the same way. His dad's tactics with his mom don't necessarily collaborate with me. Unfortunately, he never grasped this concept from my perspective.

Instead, his voice, like a broken record, repeated phrases such as, "I want to be just like my daddy... come home, sit in my chair, relax, and watch TV." And his favorite slogan, "I guess I am getting old... I go to the VA... just like my daddy." The frequent references to "my daddy" doing this or "my daddy" doing that seemed never-ending. It was clear that he longed for the comforting routine of his father; no matter the topic, the conversation always circled back to the memory of "my daddy" and, sometimes, "my mom."

As his wife, I yearned for us to create our memories and build a shared history that would unite us closer. However, his primary focus was on mirroring his father, a man who had lived a rich and charmed life. Now, it was his time to relax in his chair and watch TV, just like his father.

His actions left me feeling a deep sense of frustration and longing, as his mindset seemed somewhat selfish, not fully considering the shared experiences we could be having. This divergence in priorities became a significant obstacle, hindering our ability to create the shared history I longed for.

My husband needed to change his ways to ensure we were building and sharing great memories for ourselves and our family to reminisce on. However, we weren't bonding. Nothing transpired between us that would strengthen our relationship and create long-lasting memories.

We were stuck in a routine of emptiness, struggling to create the meaningful and lasting memories a relationship needs. We hit a plateau where both of us were yearning for more. The absence of new experiences, uncharted territories, and impromptu fun led to a decline in our shared enjoyment.

A nostalgic moment often overtakes me as my mind reverts to the past when I had nothing from the present to recall but the lack of creative memories hindering a marriage. Yet, these experiences have catalyzed personal growth, self-discovery, and accountability. They have taught me the paramount importance of shared responsibility in a relationship. Although I entertained wrongful thoughts that excluded my husband—something beyond my control because we lacked the endurance for a loving marriage—I learned that we both must own our choices, encompassing the good or bad consequences.

But why would a couple not actively create lasting memories to safeguard their marriage? I'm confident it's not intentional. It's the shared responsibility of both partners to put in extra effort to sustain a loving and exciting marriage throughout each stage of their lives while building enduring memories. Without this conscious effort, life together can become miserable, and divorce may loom in the future.

THE LOOK ON HIS FACE SAID I LOVE YOU
But He Showed Only Politeness

The morning sun glanced through my window, nudging me to wake up and start my new day. I anticipate a great beginning as I follow my usual routine: waking up, choosing my outfit for the day, washing my face, and brushing my teeth. Then, I head toward the kitchen for breakfast.

On my way, I pass my dad, who's already up and about, watching TV on the sofa. Mom is in the kitchen preparing breakfast. Suddenly, I heard an intense and loud voice asking, "Did I sleep with you last night?" I turn slowly and look around, seeing no one else in the room but my dad and me.

"Obviously." He is talking to me, but he doesn't call my name, so I continue what I am doing. He repeats, "Do you hear me talking to you?"

I turn and look around again but this time, I answer, "Yes, sir."

He asks again, "Did I sleep with you last night?" At first, I didn't understand why he was asking such a question. He knows he did not sleep with me last night. I'm thinking to myself, *why is he asking me that?*

"Since I didn't sleep with you last night, and this is the first time I saw you this morning, what should you say?" he asks.

"Good morning," I say.

And he replies, "Good morning." My father, with his calm and patient demeanor, intentionally taught me proper manners and how to be polite.

During the first several months of my marriage, my husband exhibited a beautiful routine. He would quietly get out of bed and dress himself for work. Before leaving the house, he would say, "Good morning," and kiss me goodbye. The gentle kiss on my forehead was a tender symbol of his love, and saying good morning was a reflection of the warmth and politeness his parents had instilled in him.

However, a noticeable change occurred as time passed and problems began to surface in our marriage. My husband stopped sleeping with me and moved to a separate bedroom, yet he always remembered his manners. He seemed oblivious to how his good morning which became a daily struggle for me, a constant reminder of the growing tension in our relationship that I had to carry with me throughout the day.

I couldn't get past the fact that he was not sleeping with me. The question, "Did I sleep with you last night?"—as my dad would ask—did not have the same meaning to me because this was my husband. His saying good morning to me when he was supposed to be part of my good night felt like an insult. Nonetheless, I didn't forget my manners either. I would say casually, "Hey," because I refused to say good morning.

The disparity between our actions and words made me question the authenticity of our relationship. Experiencing love reveals an intense emotional state of mind for me, encompassing spontaneity, directness, sincerity, and profoundness. Love is not a vague feeling; it is direct and clear, leaving no room for doubt. It feels emotionally offensive when the significant other declares, "I love you," but only displays politeness.

This emotional dissonance extends beyond words and gestures, seeping into the most intimate moments of a relationship. Consider this fact: A woman cannot fathom a man falling asleep during intercourse, something one would think is unheard of, but this phenomenon does occur—it goes by the name of sexsomnia, also known as somnambulistic sexual behavior. It blends elements of sleepwalking and adolescent wet dreams (Juan, 2007).

Nevertheless, a woman cannot make sense of such an act. How can a man cease making love in the middle of the performance and fall asleep while lying on top of her? The act not only violates the norms of politeness, but also inflicts emotional offense on a woman, similar to how my husband made me feel, and how many others in similar situations might feel.

From a biblical perspective, the moment when Jesus confronted the devil in the wilderness, stating, "It is written that man shall not live by bread alone, but by every word of God" (Luk. 4:4) can be analyzed as a profound parallel to our discussion. Like our discussion, this confrontation challenges the notion that love can be sustained solely by politeness. It prompts us to delve into a deeply thought-provoking question: Why did God create intimacy if that were the case? He could have easily instilled the need for one without the other.

Like comparing apples to oranges, the comparison of love and politeness mirrors our spiritual and non-spiritual bodies. Just as our human bodies require food for energy and nutrients, and our spiritual bodies need the word of God for spiritual warfare and hope, our romantic relationships, being an emotional state of mind, should also be nourished. Romantic relationships involve feeding them with spontaneity, directness, sincerity, and profoundness—always finding ways to make them personal, exciting, and unforgettable.

I am not asserting that intimacy is the primary focus in a relationship, and certainly not in a marriage. Above all, we should prioritize putting God first. In a marriage or a romantic relationship, the point is that politeness alone is not the key to a successful marriage.

My husband held my hand wherever we went. He politely opened the car door and assisted me in getting inside. He greeted me every morning with a cheerful good morning. Whenever he bought a small item for himself, such as T-shirts and electronics, he would also get one for me. He took care of cooking and cleaning. In his presence, no one could disrespect me. He spoke very highly of me and frequently gave me compliments. Around others, we were the perfect couple, always smiling, laughing, and enjoying ourselves.

Some saw me as having everything a woman might desire, but emotionally, I was starving. My husband disregarded my longing for intimacy, a crucial piece of our marriage that I felt deprived of. *Why wasn't I enough for him to address the issue that plagued my heart?*

Please understand that I appreciate the polite gestures. However, if the walls had eyes, everyone could see what transpired behind closed doors: a division that shouldn't exist between a husband and a wife. This division was not just physical, but also emotional and psychological, creating a distance that was hard to bridge. We lived like roommates and behaved like buddies inside our home.

In public, we conveyed that we loved each other through our actions and expressions to others, but at home, we were only cordial and polite.

I genuinely believe there was love between us, but certainly not enough to overcome the problems. I desired a relationship with touching, kissing, pillow talk, spontaneity, directness, sincerity, and profoundness, while he was only content with good manners and politeness.

In his song "Put That Woman First," R&B singer Jahiem expresses it well. The first contributor to the song states, "This is an ode to the importance of a woman in a relationship and the fact that she is meant to be loved and treated with respect too" (NderituPiusll, 2015).

I appreciate this observation because the contributor acknowledges that the focus is not on respect alone but on both love *and* respect.

Some of the lyrics of the song are:

[Chorus]
When she starts bringin' up old dirt
And the fights keep getting worse (Oh, brother)
Findin' numbers in her purse
Better put that woman first (Yeah)
And you know she ain't wearin' her ring (Oh, no)
When she starts playin' little games
Comin' in late from work
You better put that woman first

[Part of Verse 2]

But silly me, silly me, babe
Tell me how could I ever forget to be your lover
Now I realize that you need love too

Spend my life makin' love to you

Oh, girl

Oh, I forgot to be your lover.

My husband forgot to play the role of my lover, and the worst part was that he didn't consider it a priority. When my behavior began to change, he ignored it. Everything else went downhill from that point forward because politeness was all he was willing to give.

LEARN FROM MY MISTAKES
Prenuptial Agreement

A s I reflect on my life, one key consideration stands out. The big picture is this: I hold a well-paying job, have excellent credit and a house, just as I did before I chose to marry the man of my dreams. Like any newlywed couple, we envision prosperity as we unite. We plan to face adversities together because of our love for each other, especially since we are mature adults at fifty-plus.

However, just in case things don't go as planned, I need to know, before saying I do, if I can keep the house without any issues if we decide to part ways since I have one and he does not. With the added challenge of potential financial and emotional strain, starting over can be difficult at our age. The goal is not just to avoid any long, drawn-out legal battles over the house, but to seek a peaceful and fair resolution.

I still remember the feeling when he said, "You don't have to worry about that. I love you and would never try to take the house from you. I was married before, and when the relationship was over, I left with nothing but my clothes and a few small items to start my life over. And I will do the same thing again if necessary." His words were like a warm blanket on a cold night, comforting and reassuring, still echoing in my mind.

He spoke those sweet words from his heart at the beginning of our relationship. But the contrast between then and now hits hard with the harsh reality that those were just words. After moving out, he boldly stated, "I've filed for a divorce. My lawyer said you could sell or refinance the house to pay the value owed to me." The emotional distress of this situation was overwhelming.

"What do you mean by selling or refinancing the house?" I asked, my voice trembling with a mix of frustration, fear, and confusion.

He replied, "Don't you think I deserve something for the time and money I spent while living there?"

It suddenly became evident that trusting him to be true to his word was a fatal mistake. He expected me to sell the house and give him 50 percent of the funds because we legally lived in a community property state.

To help me understand the situation, my lawyer explained that community property laws originated when wives didn't work outside the home. Instead, they stayed home, tending to the house and children, with no monetary benefits to claim in case of divorce. The law is to help women in this situation.

Several decades later, women are tending to the home, children, and their husbands and working to help pay the bills—a legitimate reason for this law to change! These outdated laws feel like an unjust punishment that doesn't fit the reality of our contributions. It's high time for these laws to reflect the current reality.

My husband's actions left me feeling devastated and frustrated, mainly due to the financial strain. His refusal to work extra hours or get a part-time job during hard times and his last-minute payment of utilities after my unemployment and severance funds ended left me in a difficult position. His reliance on laws rather than endurance, hard work, and his words feel like a personal attack, causing a rush of emotions, headaches, and stress.

I grew up with the belief, "If at first you don't succeed, try again." In my younger days, this situation would not have fazed me. But, being close to retirement age, I've risked my heart and the things I have achieved for nothing while adding becoming emotionally drained to the list.

The relationship lacked all the expected benefits of marriage: communication, intimacy, openness, the ability to resolve conflicts, and the ability to be ourselves in each other's presence. I find myself emotionally bruised, hurt, betrayed, and rejected. As a result, I've concluded that those who are 50-plus and considering marriage should learn from my mistake and obtain a prenuptial agreement. This legal document can provide a sense of security and reassurance, outlining the terms of your marriage and protecting your assets.

Our experiences are not coincidental. Sometimes, pain helps us reach our ordained destination when we apply what we've learned. And with a prenuptial agreement, you can oversee these potential pitfalls with confidence and clarity.

My advice is: don't let kind and sweet words convince you that your spouse will not reconsider the original plan. By taking proactive steps to protect yourself with a prenuptial agreement, especially when you are over 50, you are empowering yourself and taking control of your future. This will allow you to move on in life with dignity, and that sense of empowerment will be most satisfying when you say goodbye.

I am thankful that my thinking does not align with the world's. I've asked God to examine my heart in this situation and grant me favor so I do not lose what I've accomplished. I trust him, and I believe that he will. And, as of today, God has done just that—he has granted me favor.

LIFE REALITIES
Shattered Emotions

Heartbreak can strike with devastating force, leaving deep scars on our hearts and minds. Various forms of heartbreak shatter emotions, inflicting unique and profound pain on the human soul.

Most, if not all, of us, have experienced a romantic heartbreak, where love transforms into a source of anguish as relationships crumble, forcing individuals to wrestle with devastating fragments of once-shared dreams. As I traveled, met new people, and conveyed my experiences, I heard many stories of shattered emotions. Sharing and supporting others on this journey has taught me the enormous value of our experiences and contributions.

We are not alone in these experiences, and by communicating and helping others, we can learn to deal with and cope with the pain and find hope and healing. Let's explore as I share a few stories of shattered emotions and the empowering role of communication and support in this healing process.

The Meltdown

I stood tall, disguising my insecurities with confident talk, trying to convince myself I had everything under control. Like everyone else, my strong desire for love, affirmation, and significance drove me to avoid confronting my emotions negatively. So, I spoke with dignity, feeling akin to the little engine that could. I could because I thought I could. Little did I know, I wasn't in control; my emotions controlled me.

Internally, I was struggling with a hurt that felt beyond my comprehension. Then, in a sudden and unexpected turn of events, a fierce meltdown took over. The hurt I had been carrying inside gained control over my behavior. Tears flowed, and I found myself pouting with mucus running down my face, feeling like a scolded child. At that moment, I had an acute sense of questioning my sanity.

Suddenly, I felt a void in the love and care of my family—my children, husband, and siblings. My mind had become a carousel of negativity, spinning around every aspect of my life with the same distressing thoughts returning: *Why hasn't my child called me?* The absence of my child's calls was a heavy burden on my heart. I found myself checking my phone every hour, hoping to see a missed call. But each time, deep disappointment would wash over me, leaving me to weep in silence.

My mind was all over the place. One negative thought after another as reflections of my estranged husband suddenly appeared.

Why didn't he fight for me? Wasn't I important to him? I thought a husband is supposed to protect, provide, and profess his love for his wife.

Subsequently, the negative thoughts and stress of having one job and one source of income to maintain all the household necessities entered my mind. I questioned: *Will I be able to keep my house?* Tears filled my eyes as more uncontrollable mucus ran from my nose.

And if that wasn't enough, the family secret hidden from me revealed itself: that precious child who was always on my mind was given up for adoption many years ago. My mind flashed back to the numerous times I wanted to ask if anyone had searched to see what happened to our baby but did not for fear of causing unpleasant feelings. Surprisingly, I alone had unpleasant feelings, because no one mentioned a word about this child to me.

My wandering thoughts and prayers of the child having a new and loving family lingered within me. Then, 20-plus years later, I heard the child was among our family the whole time. All these thoughts invaded my mind like a sense of betrayal creeping in, making me question my love and trust for my family. *Why did all the people I loved betray me?* However, I was grateful that I learned the identity of the new parents and saw my prayers answered. God placed the child in good hands, parents that showered the baby with all the love needed.

Then, a horrific experience reminded me of what's more important. Several months ago, my life flashed before my eyes, just like it did when I was driving along what I called a two-lane dead man's curve on Highway 49. Suddenly, a lady in a black Mustang flew by me at 85 mph as I turned into the curve's first lane. I couldn't do anything to get out of her way! She hit the cement barrier of the second lane and bounced three feet in front of me. It was only by the grace of God that she didn't hit me. But at that moment, I saw her car crashing into me, spinning my car in circles, and ending up over the barrier. Finally, her car came to a stop.

I was so nervous that I couldn't move. I sat in my car for a few minutes, trying to calm myself down before getting out to see if she was hurt. The aftermath was a blur of flashing lights, sirens, and concerned faces. But that night, I couldn't sleep. My mind focused on *what would happen if this or that happened? Why was she driving so fast? What if we were badly hurt? Who would take care of my family if I didn't make it?* I couldn't turn my mind off. I tossed and turned the whole night. I was exhausted by morning.

With all the troubling thoughts, I was drained and sinking into a place I did not belong. I was having a crisis. Thank God, I realized where I was heading. *Oh, no,* I thought. *This pity party is over!* And, as the old Chinese saying goes, "With every crisis lies an opportunity, depending on how you look at it." I started to look at each emotion differently. After all, if you can't change the situation, you should change how you think about the problem, right? Isn't that what the

Bible says? "Do not be conformed to this world, but continuously be transformed by the renewing of your minds so that you may be able to determine what God's will is—what is proper, pleasing, and perfect" (Rom. 12:1).

My firm belief and faith in agreeing with God's Word, a beacon of hope in the darkest of times, allowed me to renew my thinking and change my attitude. The near-death experience made me realize the fragility of life and the importance of cherishing every moment. It shifted my perspective, and helped me reevaluate my thoughts and priorities.

Just imagine pondering over thoughts like, *What if I had done this?* or, *Why didn't I do that?* This only serves to prolong the inevitability of depression. So, I made a firm declaration: "Emotions will not control me. Instead, I will make decisions based on wisdom, leading me toward a loving, discerning, and thriving environment." My faith, trust, and the renewal of my thinking turned my life around. I averted the disaster, and not a moment too soon!

Meaningful Relationships

A coworker's heart is saddened when he overheard a group of guys laughing and bragging about the number of relationships they have encountered during their marriages—ranging from ten-plus years to others lasting 30-plus years. Each guy expressed confidence that their wife would never leave them.

One guy declares, "Man, I come and go as I please, and my wife never says a word. As long as I pay the bills, give her a few extra dollars, and treat her special on the holidays, she couldn't care less about what I do."

Another guy chimes in, "My wife feels the same way. She tells me to do as I please but warns me not to bring home any diseases. Of course, she makes me bathe, not shower, before getting in bed with her!" he says with a smirk. "Then, she sniffs every part of my body when I get out of the tub for approval before making love with me!" *If she only knew*, I think to myself.

Man, all of y'all are crazy!" the other guy declares. "Never change your routine with your wife, and she will never suspect a thing. She will love your dirty drawls!"

A fourth guy confesses, "I cheat because my wife, the sweetest person walking this earth, does not relate to my desires, goals, aspirations, or stimulate me in any way. But I love her and can never see myself leaving her, nor do I see her leaving me, ever!"

Seated across the table from the group, the coworker walks over and says, "I couldn't help but hear the conversation you guys are having. I can relate to every point made, and if you don't mind, I would like to share how I felt after experiencing the same thoughts as you guys."

"Sure, have a seat," the guys agree.

"Thanks, guys. I appreciate it. Listen carefully, and understand that I am sharing my life story because I don't want any of you to make the same mistakes I did. I cheated because I could, without my wife uttering a word. I paid the bills, gave her anything she wanted, including sex, and was with her on special occasions. I protected myself so I did not bring disease or harm to her. I came home at a decent hour, respecting her as my wife. I helped around the house, doing the man-thing, and never changed my routine. I had everything I needed in a wife, but I didn't realize cheating was unnecessary until it was too late."

One of the guys retorted, "Oh, he's an old dude, coming over here with a sad story. None of us want to hear a gloomy story!"

"No, man, let the dude talk. I would like to hear his story," another guy said.

The coworker continued his story. "I grew up in an era when men were taught they weren't men unless they had more than one woman. My uncles demonstrated it and showed how they kept the women in check without them ever suspecting a thing. A few of them had a whole family—a woman and three children—on the side without their wives ever knowing. So, I learned from the best of them. However, I only saw the men's point of view. I never saw what the women were feeling or thinking.

"It was a rude awakening. My heart was broken with her swift and unexpected departure, leaving me in a whirlwind of emotions.

Once vibrant and promising, a love lay shattered like fragile glass. The pain surged through me as I faced the sudden end of our relationship. Every cherished memory became a haunting reminder of what once was.

"I navigated the ruins of our love, attempting to make sense of the fragments of dreams that now cut deep. The echoes of her goodbye lingered in the air, and I found myself engulfed in the bittersweet aftermath of a love that had slipped through my fingers."

"Man, that's deep," commented one of the guys. "What caused her to leave?"

"She expressed her desire for a bond that went beyond superficial interactions. In a committed partnership, she passionately believed that sharing vulnerabilities, dreams, and fears was crucial for mutual understanding and growth. She was tired of a mediocre relationship, and too many years had passed. She wanted to spend the rest of her life with someone whose words consistently reflected honesty and loyalty, building a solid foundation of trust between them. Her conviction is deeply rooted in her belief that true fulfillment in a relationship is not just about shared experiences but also about the emotional closeness that requires a connection on a profound level, which she did not have with me."

Like the old saying, "The cat got your tongue," all the guys fell silent and gloomy. A few of the guys thought, *she knew her worth, and her thoughts and outlook were profound.* Now, they all comprehended why the coworker wanted to share his story. Some began to feel remorseful and contemplated whether they should change their thinking to avoid romantic heartbreak and shattered emotions.

The small and unnoticeable things are often our life's most meaningful and powerful reflections. Therefore, we must open our minds and hearts to listen to other experiences. The coworker's words left an impression, prompting the men to reflect deeply on their actions and the value of their relationships.

Abuse

Regret in relationships can cause damage and emotional devastation, but we must also acknowledge that abusive relationships profoundly impact those involved and have lasting effects.

During a Christian group discussion, I saw a woman describe the abuse she endured after coming home from the store and how she initially mistook it for love. As she shared her story, my heart broke, and silent tears welled up as I realized the depth of her psychological and emotional trauma.

Her vivid recounting of the story continued to unfold, painting a touching picture of the day her life changed forever. "I was holding my one-year-old daughter in my left arm, with a bag of items from the Dollar Store across my right arm. As I inserted the key to unlock the front door, I used my back to push the door slightly open. Turning around, I stepped inside, and suddenly, BAM! I didn't see it coming. Behind the door was a knuckle sandwich with my name written on it.

"He smacked me so hard that I stumbled sideways into the wall, hitting my face in the same spot where he punched me, all while holding onto my baby. The pain was so excruciating that, for a moment, I lost my train of thought.

"What did I ask you to do? Did you forget?" he asked. "The only thing you are good at is spending money. And you are too stupid to realize how important it is for you to do as I ask so I can provide for this family! What must I do to get you to help out around here?"

All I could say was, "Babe, I'm sorry! I'll do it right now!" I didn't know he'd be home early. I went to the store to get what I needed and thought I'd be back in time to do what he asked. Instead, I'd disappointed him again.

He took our daughter from my arms, kissed her, and sat her on the sofa. Then, holding my face between his hands, he said, "I'm sorry too, babe. I shouldn't get angry when things don't go my way."

"When did our relationship become so unhealthy?" she wondered aloud. She believed her husband loved her. No one else saw his other side: the gentleness, caring, and attentiveness that made her feel safe. The romance and lovemaking swept her off her feet. Yet, she found herself in a constant battle, struggling to resolve this with the disrespect and violence that also came from the same person.

He claimed he was "working on" controlling his temper. However, it happened many times afterward, and she repeatedly forgave him. She believed she provoked him and that, because of her behavior, he was the victim, not her.

She continued to explain, "It amazes me when I look back and realize how vulnerable I've become. I used to feel beautiful, loved, secure, and invincible. There wasn't anything I couldn't do once I committed to it. Maybe that was the problem—my dedication to this relationship through the good and bad times.

"My family and friends knew something was wrong. They saw me emotionally deteriorate and felt there was nothing but disaster coming. It is written all over your face, they said. But, distracted by love, and because he was my husband, I let him convince me that my family and friends were jealous of us. COMPLETELY BRAINWASHED—that's what it was! I couldn't see anything through, past, or around him! Mentally, I couldn't turn back. We had to make it work. And now, all I feel is defeat, ugliness, undesirability, fear, shame, and loneliness.

"Several other incidents occurred, and it was worse each time. Finally, I didn't care what would happen. *My husband could kill me, and that would be fine with me!* I thought. I didn't want to live like that anymore because *this can't be love, can it?*

"As I sat there gazing at the TV and meditating on my situation day after day, the news became more vivid than ever before. I listened to a newscast of a woman with five kids who was involved with a guy who had shot her in the face, leaving her blind. Not long after that, I overheard some ladies in the store talking about a husband who hired "thugs" to throw lye in his wife's face just because she ended their relationship. And yet another story of a woman's boyfriend who had gouged her eyes, fractured her jaw, and broken her nose.

"Suddenly, I realized any of these stories could be me. I wanted to die, but what if I lived? How could I, this defeated, ugly, undesirable, fearful, shameful, and alone woman, live with blindness, fractured jaws, or a broken nose?

"The survival stories of these women captivated my interest. I was determined to learn more about them. My online search led me to more distressing tales. Yet, the courage of these women who had braved such experiences truly inspired me and instilled hope. Their stories prompted me to reassess my life and devise a plan to escape the relationship before it was too late. It was a decision that would prove to be one of the best I ever made. It saved my life.

"Finally, I understood what love meant. Anybody can be impressive during good times, but facing adversity is how you measure a person's intent. If a person's love only entails abuse and apologies, it will never be a healthy relationship because real love should build you up, not tear you apart, literally."

She concluded her story with crucial advice: "If you notice your self-esteem chipping away, feel isolated from your loved ones, or find yourself controlled by someone else, it's vital to recognize this as manipulation. Please seek professional help and break free before it's too late! Remember, you are a precious gem. Don't let anyone diminish your worth!"

The lady's experience and words of wisdom resonated deeply within the Christian group. She revealed yet another form of shattered emotions, recognizing that freedom from such a toxic cycle requires immense courage. But with the reassurance of support, you can find the strength to break free.

Let her words guide you. Share your experiences, for in doing so, we all become valued and heard, strengthening the bonds of our supportive community. Remember, we are in this together.

Absentee Father

The absence of a father can leave a profound void, one that shapes a child's emotional landscape in painful and lasting ways. One of my close friends shared a unique heartbreak that was unfamiliar to me. She recalls knowing that her father lived ten minutes away from her and her mom, but he displayed no interest in seeing or visiting her, which felt particularly odd given that she was an only child.

She reminisces about her parents' separation when she was eight. The memory is so vivid that she can still hear her mom's voice calling her to come and go with her while her dad was outside, diligently working under the hood of his car on a beautiful, warm day.

However, the day's beauty starkly contrasted with the internal turmoil. Her father's words, "You don't have to go with her," echoed in her mind. Despite the uncertainty, she chose to leave and go with her mom. Afterward, and unfortunately, she can't recall her father ever visiting her, leaving her with painful and lasting memories while growing up.

A few years passed, and she recalls only encountering or briefly conversing with her father, who never expressed that he loved her during her visits to her grandparents. She grew up in a one-room garage studio in the backyard of her grandparents' house. Her father, she remembers, occupied the entire 200-square-foot studio, a challenging living situation that he navigated with resilience, making the most of the limited space.

As the story goes, her father, a dedicated security police officer in the Air Force, was concluding his military service in Vietnam when he met her mom at a dance during her first year of college. They married within four months, and my friend was born a few months later. She was "daddy's little girl."

While in Vietnam, her father encountered a few close calls, including being just a few feet from enemy fire near his barracks. Although the concept of PTSD (Post-Traumatic Stress Disorder) didn't exist during Vietnam, the family believes her dad went through it, even though he chose not to get diagnosed.

Whether the strained relationship resulted from PTSD or his decision to distance himself from his only child, the fact remains that wounds of shattered emotions persist within her heart. For some unforeseen reason, she struggles to comprehend the drastic change with her father. She conceals unwelcoming thoughts such as, *How do I manage this? Why me?* But the struggle is real and ongoing.

She remembers visiting her grandparents and yearning to see her father. Deliberately, she headed to the backyard, climbed the stairs to the studio garage apartment, and knocked on the door. But she could only engage with her father for a few seconds through the screen door, depending on whether he chose to respond.

Despite his consistent lack of kindness, she persisted in her efforts to connect with him. Wounded by a broken heart and insecurities, she embraced a life of settling for less and went through periods of being promiscuous despite being an intelligent, talented, and gifted young lady, simply because she felt rejected. Her longing for her father's attention was a deep, unfulfilled need that tarnished her younger years.

Despite the pain of her father's absence, her mother's unwavering support provided a foundation that allowed her to rise above her struggles. She expresses much gratitude to her mom for nurturing her upbringing, enabling her to actively participate in school and church, cultivate goals and aspirations, and most importantly, have unwavering faith in her dreams.

Over the years, specific events in her life still trigger overwhelming emotions. As she approached her college graduation, she talked with a male friend who had also faced relationship issues with his father. This conversation rekindled feelings of frustration and anger that swept through her like a tornado when she considered her father's lack of involvement in her life or recognition of her as his child.

After careful consideration, she was determined to capture her father's attention by composing a final letter detailing her hurt and pain, giving him an ultimatum to respond or she would cease her attempts to reach out. Sadly, and to no avail, even though she poured her heart out, there was still no response for a closer relationship.

His silence did not deter her. She bravely seized control of her life and emotions. With unwavering courage, she refused to let his choices dominate her world. She separated her life from his, containing the pain to move forward. By freeing her mind from his influence, she made the bold decision that he would no longer have power over her emotions. He was as good as gone in her mind, and with that realization, she found a new sense of empowerment.

In her 20s and 30s, she embraced the roles of a wife and a mother. Thoughts of her father became sporadic, and anger no longer consumed her. She adopted the mindset of, *it is what it is. He is who he is. He is where he is, and I can do nothing about it.* This shift brought a profound sense of peace.

She acknowledged that the constant need to seek him out was not her responsibility. Instead, she set a boundary, understanding that he should want to reach out to her, his only child. With newfound clarity, she embraced her boundaries, allowing acceptance to replace the anger that had once consumed her.

So, in her early 30s, she consciously decided to revisit him. The attempt did not develop into a relationship. Still, she no longer took it personally, as she accepted the situation, reminding herself to move forward, live her life, and occasionally check on him when she could. After all, he was still her father.

Fast-forward to her 40s, she continues with a similar approach, maintaining some distance but inquiring about or visiting him occasionally. During one visit, she noticed his 6'2" stature appearing somewhat different. She inquires if he needs food and offers to make arrangements for him to eat for a while. His responses include, "Thank you," "God will bless you," and, "You don't have to come back." The last response strikes her as odd and perplexing, leaving her with a lingering sense of confusion. She wondered why he would say that, but she could do nothing about his responses.

Sometime later, she decides to take her young daughter to visit him as his only grandchild, but the reception is also lukewarm. I can only imagine her mixed emotions, wondering if he would accept her and, if not, how to explain to her daughter what she has experienced her whole life.

For many years, other family members expressed he had a mental illness and should go to the VA hospital, but he wasn't partaking in any part of it. But his demeanor and answers were coherent, bright, and clear, leaving her feeling he was not crazy. Although the war impacted his mind and how he lived, he was indeed an able body.

She didn't ask why he never said he loved her or ask any whys concerning her at all. In her mind, *it is what it is*, so she continued to move forward with her life and explained to her daughter the complexities of her grandfather.

During one of her final visits to him, she feels compelled to ask him about his health, heart, spirituality, mind, etc. She doesn't remember why she chose to do it on that particular day. But it was her intuition that proved right because shortly after that, she learned her father had been struggling with health issues he hadn't disclosed.

A few years after these events and others, her father succumbed to death where he lived, which was shocking to her. She was left to manage the autopsy, clean the scene, plan his funeral, participate in newspaper interviews, and organize a grand memorial suitable for a veteran who was also the first full-time African American police officer in Arlington, Texas. What a momentous task for her to assume!

Reflecting on her biological father sadly overtakes her at times. She regrets not experiencing him as she should have, and the sadness lingers. Her greatest disappointment stems from his death without acknowledging her as his own. There are moments when she looks at pictures, recognizing all his potential, and feels no sadness. It is what it is, and she has learned to accept what she cannot change, the true meaning of the Serenity Prayer: *God, grant me the serenity to accept the things I cannot change, courage to change the things I can, and wisdom to know the difference* (attributed to Niebuhr, 1930s). Taking ownership of knowing her worth and discovering her own confidence, she embarks on a journey to conquer her shattered emotions, leading to self-acceptance and empowerment, fueled by the courage to change what she can.

I am pleased to report that my friend witnessed God's handiwork in bringing a man into her mother's life who fulfilled every aspect of the fatherly role, proving beneficial for her when she needed it the most. In her mid-20s, he and her mom met, married, and have been together for over 25 years. Their commitment shows that God's blessings are not exclusive to one somebody but shared as they create a loving family built on love.

It also serves as a powerful reminder of how God, through faith, guides us and supports us as we navigate life's challenges, as my friend moved forward from the heartbreak of her absentee biological father.

As I conclude, the comforting words of (Rom. 8:28) serve as a reassuring reminder of God's plan and purpose in our lives. "*And we know that all things work together for good to them that love God, to them who are the called according to his purpose.*"

Siblings

Deteriorating bonds among siblings can become increasingly upsetting, slowly widening like a crack in a foundation until once-solid relationships crumble into battlegrounds of unresolved conflict. This conflict can profoundly impact us, leaving behind a deserted trail of resentment and bitterness that conceals the light of family bonds.

Much like an urgent intervention, a call to action for understanding and healing is in sight. The urgency of this situation cannot be overstated. Without the relief of mutual understanding, tensions can flare like wildfire, consuming everything in its path. We must recognize the situation's urgency and the need for immediate intervention to prevent further damage, knowing that the healing potential is always present.

The following situation is all too familiar to some of us. A coworker shared her family's heartbreak as they struggled to divide the proceeds from their parents' property sale among the three siblings. They were overwhelmed with emotions, and frustration was boiling over as accusations flew back and forth. With a glare, her older sister accused her of manipulating the situation for personal gain. Her brother, defiant, argued for what he believed was his rightful share, demanding it without delay. The older sister, however, insisted on holding out for a higher offer based on market value before finalizing the settlement, fully aware of the financial implications. She refused to sign any documents until she received a better price, using her strong financial position to afford the luxury of waiting. With a dismissive tone, she declared, "I'm not using the same lawyer. I've hired my own."

Suddenly, the chaos evaporated, leaving the room in tense silence. No one said a word. The brother and her frowns mirrored each other. They shared the same thoughts and storm of frustration. *Who does she think she is? Better than us? The clock is ticking—now is the time to settle. We all have needs, and the money can't come soon enough!*

Despite her frustration, calmly, she reminded her siblings of the importance of their unity, saying, "We should consider that the process could become complicated if the property enters probate, faces disputes, or encounters delays. If expenses or debts are due, the court might order the sale of the property to cover costs, possibly leading to a lower-than-expected price. This risk should make us all cautious to avoid further delays. Our unity is crucial in navigating through the process."

The coworker and her brother were willing to accept the original offer. However, the room remained tense as they struggled to find common ground with their oldest sister.

As anticipated, since they could not reach an agreement, the property entered probate, further prolonging the process. Over the next six months, this created a strained atmosphere and unnecessary family heartbreaks, deteriorating their bond. The probate process began a year ago, and the matter remains unresolved.

With a mediator's guidance, the outcome might have been different, leaving no trail of resentment and bitterness in its wake. Once the property sale is complete, perhaps the siblings can resolve their issues by embracing open communication and, most importantly, setting aside their differences.

Knowing that the siblings couldn't resolve the matter beforehand is heartbreaking. Still, by actively listening to each other's perspectives and working toward a common goal, they can transform conflicts into opportunities for growth.

It's important to remember that the ultimate goal is to preserve strong and supportive family ties. Through compromise and mutual respect, they can find solutions that benefit everyone, reinforcing their commitment to each other and the family.

Friendships

Once again, we recognize the diverse nature of emotional pain. Betrayal or fading connections cut deep, leaving individuals to navigate the void of a once—shared bond. These emotions ring especially true when the heartbreak of a friendship cuts as deeply as that of family ties.

Although this happened long ago in high school, I watched as the once inseparable bond between two girls unraveled over a guy. Sharon and Bonita, who had shared secrets and dreams, drifted apart when the charismatic newcomer, Tony, arrived.

Captivated by Tony's attention, Sharon began spending more time with him, unintentionally sidelining Bonita. It was not her intention to hurt her friend, but the allure of Tony was too strong to resist. Meanwhile, Tony, who was friendly with both girls, had no issue talking with each of them as friends.

Tensions escalated as both girls found themselves in a complex situation and developed feelings for Tony. Unaware of Bonita's growing resentment, Sharon continued seeking Tony's company, unknowingly and rapidly widening the gap in their friendship.

Her frustration boiled over as she confronted Bonita in the hallway. "You can't just swoop in like this, Bonita! Tony and I were getting close, and now you're all over him. It's not cool."

Bonita said defensively, "I'm not 'swooping in,' Sharon. We can't control who we like. I didn't ask for this, and you can't claim ownership over someone's feelings."

Sharon's voice trembled with hurt as she said, "Ownership? We were supposed to be best friends, Bonita. You know how much I liked him, and you're acting like it doesn't matter. It's like you don't care about our friendship at all. I feel so betrayed!"

Bonita's eyes narrowed. "I care, but I can't suppress my feelings for your sake. Maybe you should have been more upfront about your feelings for Tony instead of assuming he'd naturally be yours. I'm not the bad guy here."

Tension filled the air as their argument echoed through the crowded hallway, making the strain on their friendship palpable. Unable to reconcile their conflicting emotions and desires, the once-close friends found themselves on opposite sides of a romantic triangle. Unspoken feelings and the magnetic pull of a shared crush gradually eroded their bond, slowly chipping away at the trust that once held them together as best friends.

In the end, while their once sibling-like friendship faded, the lessons learned from such experiences remind us that growth and maturity can guide us through similar challenges in adulthood. With time and self-awareness, we can navigate conflicts more thoughtfully, preserving relationships and building a stronger, more connected foundation for the future.

For those who believe in the Bible, remember what is said in Luke. So watch yourselves! "If another believer sins, rebuke that person; then if there is repentance, forgive. Even if that person wrongs you seven times a day and each time turns again and asks forgiveness, you must forgive" (Luk. 17: 3-4).

We can overcome the challenges that strain our relationships by embracing growth, maturity, and forgiveness. Whether guided by personal values or biblical teachings, the willingness to forgive and rebuild trust ensures that even fractured bonds have the potential to heal and strengthen over time.

Losing a Loved One

Life certainly has its ways of unleashing an overwhelming wave of shock and grief that disrupts one's sense of stability. Navigating through the waves of sadness, confusion, and emptiness, we find ourselves on a journey of coming to terms with the harsh impact of loss. This journey, filled with uncontrollable emotions and heartbreak, is a challenging but necessary part of our healing process.

As I reflect on my grandmother, memories flood back like a bittersweet melody. In her cozy room, a haven of comfort that always felt like a warm embrace, I recall holding her frail yet strong hand, watching tears well up in her eyes and seeing the pain etched across her face as she lay in bed. Nostalgia and the looming shadow of loss filled the air, wrapping around us like a sad song that lingers long after its final note.

My grandmother, once vibrant and full of life, lay on the bed, her body weakened by the relentless passage of time. Despite the approaching end, an undeniable warmth filled the room—a love transcending the physical realm.

Memories flooded my mind like a cherished photo album, each page unfolding with laughter, the stories told, and the countless moments intertwined with our strong bond. From scratching dandruff from her thin, silver hair to preparing home-cooked meals for me as a young adult working in downtown Houston, only 15 minutes from where she lived, she eagerly awaited my lunch break. It was a time for us to share in the joy of our conversation, to relax in the happiness and positivity of our bond.

As my grandmother's breaths grew increasingly shallow, I realized I needed to call 911, and devastation quickly gripped my emotions. I found solace in the touch of her weathered hands—the same hands that had cradled me as a child, wiped away my tears, and soothed my fears.

I dialed 911, and the ambulance quickly arrived, carrying her away. My intuition told me she would not return. Shortly after, I received the call confirming my fears—my grandmother had suffered a heart attack and passed away.

A wave of emotions—hurt, pain, and loss—overwhelmed me, flooding my heart with an indescribable mix of sorrow and gratitude. I knew the love we shared would forever be knitted into the fabric of my soul, a lasting tribute to the extraordinary woman whose enduring influence shaped me into the person I am today. This tribute will always be a part of me.

Yet, as I braced myself to cope with the shattered emotions, I faced extreme sadness, confusion, and emptiness, knowing that healing would take time. In that moment of deep sorrow, I found solace in my personal growth and drew strength from the belief that the Lord stays close to the brokenhearted and rescues those with crushed spirits (Pslm. 34:18). This belief in finding peace through faith and personal growth became my guiding light, assuring me that healing would come in time.

Illness

Receiving an illness diagnosis can unleash a new wave of devastating emotions as individuals face the daunting task of trying and eliminating medications to find the ones best suited for their condition.

The overwhelming pain intensifies when healthcare professionals recommend various medications, making individuals feel like guinea pigs. I can certainly attest to this feeling, having cried and felt depressed as I started with one illness only to seem to acquire many more due to the medications. Hopefully, by sharing personal experiences like mine, we can shine a light on the emotional storm triggered by healthcare recommendations.

While I maintained a tolerant expression and projected strength outwardly, inside, I was miserable, grappling with a messy mix of determination and defeat.

I will never forget how a soothing, hot shower turned into a battlefield when a wave of excruciating, unbearable pain seized my right eye. The indescribable agony left me grappling to stand upright as I searched for its cause. "Oh my God, what is this?" I cried out, fervently praying and declaring, "By Jesus' stripes, I am healed. By Jesus' stripes, I am healed. God, please! Please! Help me!"

Instantly, my faith became my anchor, my source of strength, eventually filling me with a sense of calm and resilience.

As I reexamined the incident, the pain grew like a storm, overshadowing the intensity of childbirth, stretching those few seconds into a never-ending tempest.

I felt relief when the pain finally stopped, only for it to return by the time I made it from the shower to the sofa. Once again, I screamed, passionately praying and proclaiming my healing.

The fear of being incapacitated, like a blind man crossing the streets and getting hit by a car, restricted me from sudden movements. Turning my head to the left or right or lying on my back was impossible.

By morning, I was still crying and experiencing sudden electric shocks of pain. I decided to go to the emergency room, where my daughter met me and gratefully prepared the admission paperwork as I humbled myself like a helpless newborn baby. The ER doctor conducted a CT scan that revealed no tumors. Despite being thankful for the news, concerns lingered about the pain returning.

Trigeminal neuralgia, a condition that affects the trigeminal nerve, has significantly impacted my daily life. Simple tasks like brushing my teeth, washing my face, or applying makeup can trigger intense pain. To manage this, my doctor has prescribed a treatment plan. This includes prednisone, 20 MG, to be taken orally once a day for ten days, and tramadol, 50 MG, to be taken orally every six hours if severe pain occurs, for up to five days. I was also advised to follow up with my primary care doctor in three days, highlighting the importance of ongoing care in managing this condition.

My primary care doctor prescribed chewable tablets of carbamazepine, 100 MG, twice a day. Unfortunately, this medication led to a series of adverse reactions, including extremely high blood pressure, dizziness, drowsiness, fatigue, nosebleeds, and fast heartbeats. In response, my doctor switched the medication to gabapentin, 300 MG once a day, which not only alleviated the side effects but also proved to be effective in managing my condition.

However, my immediate concern was if the medication would heal the damaged nerve. I could not imagine living the rest of my life with such excruciating pain. He explained that the trigeminal nerve would heal over time, whether it took weeks, months, or even years.

After seven months, I began experiencing sporadic headaches on the right side of my face and the top of my head. An MRI revealed damage to several blood vessels, probably due to the extremely high blood pressure, since I didn't have the issue beforehand. My primary care doctor, who closely monitored my condition and played a crucial role in my treatment plan, initiated a prescription for propranolol, starting with 40 MG tablets per week to address the migraine headaches, along with the gabapentin. If the headaches subsided, he would increase the milligrams.

While it's important to be aware, it's also crucial to remember that severe and potentially life-threatening side effects from propranolol, like many other medications, are rare. The list of potential side effects can be daunting, but it's important to remember that most people do not experience these. However, I chose not to take it due to the following possible side effects and the fact that I was already experiencing some issues with my vision as a side effect of the previous medicine.

- Signs of an allergic reaction, such as rash; hives; itching; red, swollen, blistered, or peeling skin with or without fever; wheezing; tightness in the chest or throat; difficulty breathing, swallowing, or talking; unusual hoarseness; or swelling of the mouth, face, lips, tongue, or throat.

- Signs of low blood sugar like dizziness, headache, feeling sleepy, feeling weak, shaking, a fast heartbeat, confusion, hunger, or sweating.

- Signs of lupus like a rash on the cheeks or other body parts, sunburn easily, muscle or joint pain, chest pain or shortness of breath, or swelling in the arms or legs.

- Bad dizziness or passing out.

- Chest pain which is new or worse.

- Slow heartbeat.

- A heartbeat that does not feel normal.
- Shortness of breath, big weight gain, or swelling in the arms or legs.
- Feeling confused.
- Hallucinations (seeing or hearing things that are not there).
- Memory problems or loss.
- Depression or other mood changes.
- A burning, numbness, or tingling feeling that is not normal.
- Feeling cold in the arms or legs.
- Change in color of hands, feet, or other areas. Skin may turn pale, blue, gray, purple, or red.
- Change in eyesight.
- Any unexplained bruising or bleeding.
- Fever, chills, or sore throat.

As I endured the relentless heartaches of prescription drugs and their accompanying side effects, my friends and family rallied around me. They were determined to provide comfort and solace amidst the tempest of my shattered emotions as I actively sought the best solution for my situation, considering whether I should take the drugs or not.

In conclusion, my rational intuition guided me to recognize that the risks associated with propranolol—affecting my heart and eyes, causing hallucinations, weight changes, depression, and exacerbating lupus—were too significant. This was a deeply personal decision, as the drug might alleviate my headaches, but the potential for adding numerous other issues seemed too great.

Professional

The storms of life don't just rattle windows, they can also break them, like when someone full of ambition loses all hope.

As previously demonstrated, life's challenges have the potential to create many shattered emotions, and a person's professional career does not take a back seat to these scenarios. They can be equally devastating, often leading to biased decision-making or unreasonable expectations on the job. These are workplace issues and the visible impact of personal challenges within our professional lives.

In my early twenties, tensions flared when my manager confronted me about a financial discrepancy. The conflict was not just about a significant sum of money that needed to be invested over the weekend, but about the enormous fees and interest that would follow due to the oversight, a financial burden that my superior could have avoided.

My superior's manager insisted I should bear total responsibility, which was hard to accept given my agreement with my superior to split the accounts, leaving me accountable only for those assigned to me. The pressure from this unjustified blame felt like life's storms cracking the glass, threatening to shatter it completely. The experience left me in a state of vulnerability and exposure, especially after feeling greatly appreciated when I brought the mistake to my superior's attention.

Imagine the excitement I felt when I discovered that my superior had forgotten to invest some of the money in the accounts he was responsible for in time for the weekend. I brought it to his attention, despite splitting the accounts and responsibilities, thinking I was helping. As the story unfolded, my superior and his manager decided to pin the oversight on me. I was devastated.

The professional relationship between my superior and me, which once thrived on mutual respect, now hung in the balance, fractured by the fallout and biased decision-making, an absolute contrast to the respect we once shared.

But I stood firm, refusing to take responsibility for the oversight because it wasn't right or fair. In retaliation, the manager transferred me to a different department under worse conditions, which led to my dismissal two months later—just as I approached full investment in the company.

The sudden change was not just upsetting, but it left me vulnerable and uncertain about every aspect of my life. Questions about financial stability, job prospects, and the potential impact on my professional relationships began to surface. The abrupt shift forced me to reevaluate my career path, goals, and priorities.

As I grappled with the overwhelming uncertainties and the weight of starting over in a challenging job market, I felt my confidence shatter. However, this experience was a profound lesson in resilience and the importance of standing up for what is right, even in adversity. The anger, disappointment, and the need to fight back that initially crushed my feelings ultimately became the source of my empowerment.

Later, I came to understand that life's realities, in all their forms, deeply impact the human spirit. They assess our resilience, often leaving us with the daunting task of rebuilding from the fragments of our shattered emotions. Yet, they also highlight the profound influence of courage.

This force, more potent than we often realize, empowers us to persist in our pursuit of justice, a noble cause we should never turn our backs on. It inspires us to approach our work enthusiastically, as if we were serving the Lord rather than people, believing a reward awaits us (Col. 3:23-24).

Homelessness

Sometimes, homelessness begins with a sudden loss of employment, as the security of a steady paycheck evaporates into thin air. Other times, the crushing burden of medical bills pushes individuals and families over the edge, their savings depleted in the fight for survival.

Substance abuse and mental health struggles can also play a role, turning once-stable lives into a turbulent whirlwind of uncertainty. For some, it's a matter of escaping abusive relationships, only to find themselves with nowhere to turn.

The lack of affordable housing and inadequate support systems further exacerbate the situation, leaving countless individuals staggering on the brink of homelessness with no safety net to catch them.

As these challenges pile up, the once-solid ground beneath their feet crumbles away, leaving them adrift in a world that seems to have forgotten their existence.

Unfortunately, the prospect of seeking help at a shelter can evoke a deep sense of embarrassment for those experiencing homelessness because of the stigma that fuels feelings of shame and inadequacy, leading individuals to internalize social judgments about their worth and value. They may fear others seeing them as failures or burdens on society, further isolating themselves from seeking assistance.

The vulnerability of admitting one's homelessness can feel like a loss of control over life, causing feelings of powerlessness. As individuals, we all desire to maintain a semblance of dignity. But in the face of adversity, we wrestle with the psychological toll of our circumstances, which may deter us from reaching out for help.

Social stigma, personal pride, and the struggle to maintain a sense of independence amidst adversity cause some to be reluctant to seek shelter assistance, which produces another form of heartbreak, shattered emotions, that inflicts a unique and profound pain on the human mind, body, and soul.

I must admit that thoughts of homelessness have often crossed my mind. There have been times when I wasn't sure if circumstances beyond my control would leave me without a home. The uncertainty of whether I could live with one of my siblings or either of my children was a constant source of tension.

I recall my mother saying, "Baby, try and keep your house." Her words were like a plant growing deeply in the ground. The roots play a vital role in maintaining the plant's health, yet their importance often goes unnoticed when you can't see them.

Similarly, one should not ignore my mom's wisdom based on her experience of having to live with someone else or being homeless. Her wisdom plays a vital role in the encouragement and determination of one not to give up on having your own home. Understand me when I say it is a blessing to have those who love you enough to take you in and care for you. But there is also that sense of losing your independence because the house rules and life, as you once knew, change from when you were in control, and you must adjust, which isn't always easy when considering social stigma, personal pride, and the struggle to maintain.

It's important to remember that, as individuals, we all share a common desire for dignity and independence. This shared desire is what connects us all, regardless of our circumstances. My sincere prayer is that I never have to experience losing my home, living with someone else, or becoming a homeless person. I'm sure I will do what is needed to survive, but I ask God to spare me from that experience.

Once, at a group gathering, someone brought up a homeless person using all of their money to stay in hotels because they refused to contact a shelter. It made me realize that not everyone has the luxury of family support during hard times. This was further emphasized when another group member shared that when faced with hard times, her family refused to take her and her children in. It was a stern reminder that we all need to be part of a supportive community.

She had no choice but to seek shelter assistance. She mentioned that there are a lot of excellent shelters available. Again, I wasn't aware of any excellent shelters because I did not know of them. My only knowledge of homelessness and shelters is what I see on TV and those people living under bridges.

As an outsider looking in on the situation, I can only imagine a homeless person expressing themselves as such: I feel the biting sting of uncertainty every day. The cold pavement beneath me offers little comfort as I navigate the harsh realities of life without a stable shelter. With each passing moment, the weight of isolation and invisibility presses down on me, reminding me of my place on the fringes of society. Hunger gnaws at my stomach, a constant reminder of my vulnerability in a world that often overlooks those without a home. The indifference of spectators cuts more deeply than any chill, leaving me yearning for physical and emotional warmth. Yet, amongst the struggle, there remains a flicker of resilience, a spark of hope that tomorrow might bring relief from this relentless hardship.

This notion brings to mind the contrast between selfishness and humility, as beautifully depicted in (Philippians 2:3-7). The passage advises avoiding selfish motives and the urge to impress others. Instead, it encourages us to adopt a humble attitude, considering others as superior to ourselves. It's a powerful reminder, a source of motivation and empowerment, to not only focus on our own interests but also to take an active interest in the well-being of others.

CONCLUSION
Comprehending the Experiences

───────────────────

As I conclude *Life Realities,* I am struck by how our journeys intertwine like threads in a rich tapestry of love, heartbreak, and resilience. The challenges of shattered emotions, abuse, and loss have tested our mettle. It's in these moments that our family and friends have truly shone, being our rock and providing a sense of security when the storms of life, illness, and professional setbacks raged. Their prayers and positive energy have been a constant source of strength, reinforcing our perseverance. Their honest feedback, delivered with love and faith, has sharpened our vision, fostering the resilience to face obstacles and the confidence to pursue our passions with renewed energy. Their unwavering support, encouragement, and wisdom have been a guiding light for which we are deeply grateful.

Even in the darkest moments, when we face homelessness or bid farewell to loved ones, these experiences have served us well, teaching us profound lessons in determination to move forward. They have taught us resilience and the power of hope. Today, we stand stronger, healed by time, and deeply grateful for the love and unwavering support of those who never gave up on us. As we look toward the future, we embrace the next chapter with hope, knowing that our trials have not only prepared us for joy, peace, and fulfillment but also enlightened us with the strength to rise through every challenge.

Special thanks and appreciation go to *Life Realities'* known and unknown contributors, who openly shared their journeys through life's ups and downs. Their stories empower many to share experiences to help others overcome and conquer their realities. Their stories, a powerful testament to the commonality of human experiences, foster a deep sense of connection and understanding. Remember, our shared perseverance paves the way for success, and it is a quality we all possess, connecting us as human beings.

ADVENTURES – ENJOYING THE NEXT CHAPTER
Setting Goals and Achieving Them

Welcome to *Adventures—Enjoying the Next Chapter*, where I focus on the empowering process of *Setting Goals and Achieving Them*. Through the inspiring stories shared by the contributors of *Life Realities*, I am determined to enjoy my life as I move forward, starting with lessons learned from my teachers that fuel my determination to set and achieve goals.

During career month in middle school, the teachers introduced us to the era's highest-paying career opportunities. They urged us to choose a career path and assigned classes that would help us achieve our chosen goals.

My initial goal was to find the highest-paying career, leading me to choose accounting. Little did I know then that this decision would lead me down a path I never expected. Despite not becoming an accountant, I graduated with a business degree and worked in accounting and payroll until retirement.

My career took unexpected twists, but the power of words to guide and inspire stayed constant. Famous quotes fascinate me for their ability to distill wisdom, spark action, and offer concise insights that shift perspectives and provide comfort. Their simplicity makes them easy to remember and practical to apply in daily life.

One of my favorite quotes emphasizes focusing on and achieving goals: 'The best way to predict the future is to create it.' This guiding principle helped me set and reach my career goals and now drives me toward my personal goals. Proverbs 21:5, one of my favorites, from the New King James Version, which, in my view, expresses it even better: 'The plans of the diligent lead to profit as surely as haste leads to poverty.' This verse reminds me of the power of diligence and careful planning in achieving success. It's a testament to the power of personal commitment in achieving our goals. One thing was clear: I had no desire to be poor!

When my son, now 33 years old, was in elementary school, he wrote down what he wanted to do when he grew up and placed it in a handmade mitten as a Christmas ornament. The outside read: I'M JUST A LITTLE MITTEN, BUT TUCKED INSIDE OF ME ARE MY 2002 THOUGHTS OF WHAT AGE 18 WILL BE. SO, UNTIL MY 18TH BIRTHDAY, HANG ME ON YOUR TREE AND OPEN ME ON CHRISTMAS DAY FOR A HAPPY MEMORY. Inside the mitten, he wrote: *Going to College.*

Every year we read it, smiled, and placed it on the Christmas tree. From that point forward, the mindset and goal setting were in place. He graduated from college with a Bachelor of Science Degree in

Game Development and is currently working on a degree in Biotechnology.

I share these experiences to show that writing down your goals makes you more likely to engage intellectually and connect emotionally with the result you want to achieve. Like in my career, I realized that setting personal goals requires the same focus and intention. With this understanding, I began implementing my personal goals, knowing they are not just important but crucial. My priorities are traveling, being adventurous, and seeing God's magnificent creation.

My goals are in motion, and I'm achieving them. The joy and excitement of pursuing these goals is unmistakable. I'm deeply grateful for my opportunities and those still ahead. So now, please sit back and enjoy as I share my journey.

Cancun, Mexico

My first journey to the Caribbean, which took place in captivating Cancun, Mexico, in 2002, was a tour of discovery, a fantastic first-time experience. The stunning beaches, the feeling of sand between my toes, and the vibrant local culture I immersed myself in all left a permanent mark of passion.

I exchanged currency, shopped, and enjoyed the delicious cuisine, even indulging in American fried apple pies at the unique McDonald's in Cancun, the only place where they still fry their apple pies. This trip opened my eyes to the cost-efficiency of traveling. It introduced me to the richness and diversity of different cultures, which has become a high priority in achieving my personal goals.

Copper Mountain, Colorado

My coworkers spoke highly of their family ski vacations, and at the time, I thought it was impossible for me to go. In the community where I grew up, there wasn't much talk about a Black family going skiing. There was hardly any snow. We were lucky to build a snowman every ten or fifteen years. Skiing was seen on TV only.

Still, I imagined the thrill of gliding down snow-covered slopes, the crisp mountain air, and the breathtaking winter landscapes. I was surprised to learn that Houston, Texas, has a Black ski club, and even more excited when my best friend invited me to go skiing with her, her sister-in-law, and the Black ski club, which were friends of my best friend's sister-in-law. It was an unexpected invitation and a blessing!

In 2003, we visited Copper Mountain Resort in Colorado for my first ski vacation. It was terrific, but undoubtedly different from the Caribbean. Climbing those snowy mountains at such a high altitude makes breathing hard because the air is thinner and contains less oxygen, making it harder for the body to take in the oxygen it needs.

I breathed faster and more deeply than ever before to compensate for the lower oxygen levels. My chest felt like it would cave in.

Mentally, my thoughts surfaced around whether I would make it home! However, the Black Ski Club, having done this many times, shared some valuable advice. They emphasized the importance of drinking more water and avoiding or reducing alcohol consumption to help with breathing. They also suggested taking frequent breaks to rest and adapt to the altitude. Water became my faithful companion! I had more of it than I ever had in my life.

Partying with the Black Ski Club was great, but some of my snow adventures were not. I recall feeling like the blizzard would bury me underneath the snow as I struggled alone to reach the top of the slope. Walking in the snow is much more complicated than skiing with ski shoes. The ski shoes are heavy and bulky, making lifting your feet high with each step difficult. They also sink into the snow, making it difficult to move forward. The uneven terrain and deep snow make walking exhausting and slow, especially for a beginner like me.

In contrast, skiing with ski shoes allows you to glide smoothly over the snow, distributing your weight evenly and reducing the effort needed to move. Ski shoes provide better balance and efficiency, making navigating snowy slopes easier and allowing you to enjoy the experience. But I wasn't used to ski shoes or skiing, so it was challenging. To make things worse, everyone seemed to pass me by, not even offering a word of encouragement or a helping hand when I stumbled. I remember the tears and feeling like I would never do this again.

As I hiked upwards, each step was a battle; the wind whistled and the snow swirled, threatening to consume me. The relentless blizzard seemed to suggest the fleeting nature of life. But when I finally conquered the peak, a surge of relief and triumph washed over me. I yearned for the safety of the ski lift, the stability of solid ground, and the familiarity of my room.

The thought of braving the daunting snow on foot or skis again was out of the question! Instead, I embraced the rest of the trip with tubing, lively parties, and exhilarating games of charades, a complete contrast to the challenging ski trip, bringing a sense of relief and joy.

It was a challenging journey, but it was also a journey of self-discovery and resilience. As I pushed through it, I reminded myself of the beautiful scenery and the thrill of trying to learn how to ski. I would do it again in a heartbeat!

Cozumel, Mexico

In 2004, I could hardly contain my excitement as I embarked on my traveling expeditions, eager to share every thrilling moment and discovery with my family. I took my middle-school-aged son on his first out-of-state trip to Cozumel.

The vibrant sights of colorful buildings, lush tropical plants, and clear turquoise water greeted us. The air buzzed with the lively sounds of street musicians playing traditional Mexican tunes, mingling with the laughter and chatter of fellow travelers. The tantalizing aroma of fresh seafood grilling and the fragrant scent of tropical flowers filled the air, making every moment a feast for the senses.

My son enjoyed the experience as much as I did, and has made traveling his goal ever since. However, I have yet to convince my now adult daughter to travel. I hope she will experience it and share those adventures with me before I leave this earth. Until then, I will continue to share the breathtaking beauty of the adventures of my life with her.

Carnival Cruise

The year 2004 was a year of firsts for me, including my first cruise. I found myself back in Cozumel, this time on the *Ecstasy*, a Carnival Cruise Line ship. As I approached the massive ship dock at the port, a mix of excitement and anticipation filled me. But upon boarding, the sheer size and splendor of the ship left me feeling a bit overwhelmed, like a small fish in a huge ocean.

My mind had not prepared me for the lively activities and multitude of amenities that were available. The view of the ocean alone was awe-inspiring. Like a child at a birthday party, I eagerly explored every deck, trying to get my bearings and deciding what to do first, then next, and what I would do on the ship entirely!

As I embarked on the cruise, I was immediately captivated by the numerous all-inclusive dining venues, each offering a plethora of tempting dishes. The lavish buffet breakfast, lunch, and dinner were a food lover's dream. I couldn't resist the urge to pile my plate high with all I could eat, including snacks from the various cafes and snack bars scattered around the ship. It was as if I had never seen food!

The abundance of gourmet dining options, themed dinners, and specialty restaurants made it all too easy to succumb to the allure of delicious cuisine and overeat throughout the cruise. I stuffed myself, feeling the pounds adding up. My appetite had become so pathetic that I reasoned with myself, saying it was only four days. But as the cruise went on, I couldn't help but feel a bit of regret for my lack of self-control and indulgence.

During the day, I walked the deck people watching, and I saw many strange people on the ship all having a marvelous time drinking, dancing, relaxing while suntanning, getting tattoos, and playing all sorts of games. Honestly, I didn't feel like I was on a ship. I couldn't see dry land for miles away, yet I enjoyed myself as if on land.

At night, the cruise ship transformed into a lively and vibrant scene. My friends and fellow passengers flocked to the various bars and lounges, where talented bartenders made creative cocktails and served drinks with style. The dance floors came alive with music as live bands or DJs kept the rhythm going late into the night. I mingled and socialized, making new friends as I enjoyed the entertainment.

Some of us headed to the onboard theater to catch dazzling performances, while others participated in themed parties like the Tropical Paradise or '80s Retro Night, or karaoke nights featuring popular hits from the '90s. Depending on the performances, I made sure I saw both theater and karaoke.

I'm not much on gambling, so the ship's casino did not excite me.

At the end of the night, I was mesmerized by the backdrop of the twinkling stars above and the gentle sway of the ship on the ocean waves. Cruising was such a beautiful and unforgettable experience filled with fun and excitement that I did it again for the next three years as my second vacation for the year.

Las Vegas, Nevada

I visited Las Vegas for the first time in 2005. As I mentioned before, I'm not big on gambling, but I was granted the opportunity and felt, why not?

Upon my arrival, the dazzling sights and sounds surrounding me overwhelmed my senses instantly. The neon lights illuminated the streets with a colorful glow. The loudness of slot machines, laughter, and music filled the air, creating a symphony of excitement.

The hotel casinos, each more extravagant than the last, lined the famous Strip, beckoning me to come and experience the thrill. So, I played the slot machines for a while, but never entirely adapted to gambling. I had expected to be more drawn to the gambling scene, but I found myself more intrigued by the city's other offerings. The Grand Canyon, a natural wonder, left me in awe of its beauty. The shows, with their glitz and glamour, captivated me. But unfortunately, I didn't get a chance to experience them during this visit.

Antigua and Barbuda

In 2006, with determination, I embarked on my journey to Antigua and Barbuda using a buddy pass to connect with my friends flying from Houston, Texas, to Newark, New Jersey. I planned to meet them in Houston, fly with them to New Jersey, and continue our adventure to Antigua.

As the departure time for the flight from Houston to Antigua neared, I found myself stranded in Dallas, a feeling of tension building up as I watched other passengers aboard the plane. Whenever I thought I had a secured seat, the flight filled up, leaving me scrambling for another option. My friends and I were in constant and crucial communication, a lifeline in this uncertain situation, trying to figure out the next-best move if I were to miss the flight to Houston.

The unpredictability turned my plan for an exciting trip into a stressful ordeal. My brother-in-law, as I called him, was one of my best friends' husbands. He decided to meet me halfway between Dallas and Houston to reach the airport in time to board the plane to Newark. His wife and the others on the trip would also meet us at the airport. My sister drove me to Centerville, the halfway point to Houston, and we began our journey.

At first, everything was working out well. But then, a car accident caused a massive backup, trapping us and countless others in a sea of brake lights. The drivers around us grew increasingly impatient, honking their horns and trying to maneuver into an imaginary, slightly faster lane.

With every passing minute, our plans for the day slipped away, and the radio's traffic updates offered little hope for a quick resolution. However, my brother-in-law, a man of immense faith and unwavering determination, believed we would make it in time for the flight. He began ducking in and out of traffic, crossing over to the side of the road, driving through back roads, and then returning to the freeway. Finally, just in time, we reached our destination. Thank you, Jesus!

We all made it to Newark, but the same frustrating sequence of events with the buddy passes cost us a full day of our four-day trip to Antigua. We spent the night at the airport, waiting for the next available flight. The experience was far from pleasant, with uncomfortable seats, constant announcements over the loudspeaker, and the continuous movement of other travelers.

The harsh fluorescent lights overhead made it impossible to relax, and the hard, cold floor offered no comfort. Despite our exhaustion, we could not find a position that allowed us to rest, and each passing hour felt like a lifetime as we longed for the comfort of our beds. We eventually had to accept that a decent night's sleep was out of reach until we could board our flight.

Finally, we arrived at the resort, and its enchanting charm captivated us immediately. The scent of the colorful flowers and the sound of the birds chirping in the lush greenery of the meticulously landscaped gardens highlighted the resort's beauty.

As we walked through the fascinating entrance, the warm staff members greeted us and guided us to our spacious rooms. A few of us enjoyed a stunning view of the sandy white beach, while others had to walk outside the room and onto the beach to enjoy the sight. Either way, the view was magnificent.

But just as we settled in, an unexpected turn for tourists occurred: it started to rain. This unforeseen weather condition forced us to postpone our plans, causing us to lose half a day exploring the resort and the island. However, this twist of fate led us to a thrilling encounter with a local guide on the plane. A resident of Antigua and a tourist guide for the island, he offered to take us exploring the land and its city lifestyle. As soon as the rain subsided, we began our venture, filled with the excitement of the unexpected.

As we drove through the city streets, we encountered an unusual sight: chickens, cows, and other animals leisurely crossing our path. The tourist guide stopped as if it were the legal, not the common-sense, thing to do. This unique cultural experience immediately captured my attention.

In a playful manner, I asked, "Do you also stop for snakes to cross the road?"

The response I received was unexpected. "We don't have snakes. We import mongoose, known for their fearless attacks on highly venomous snakes, to hunt and keep them in check." These mongooses' audacity, fearless nature, and the city's ingenious approach to snake control left me genuinely impressed.

Despite the grandeur of the city's dwellings, there was little else to stir our excitement of the city lifestyle. So, after the tour, we eagerly embraced the resort's attractions for the remaining two and a half days, yearning for a trouble-free journey back. We were fortunate to have just that—a journey home as smooth as silk, with no hiccups or issues with the buddy passes.

Jamaica

The Caribbean, a haven of beauty and tranquility, is also a hub of adventure and excitement. The islands are surrounded by clear waters, powdery white sands, and lush green palm trees that gently sway in the breeze, casting inviting shadows on beach umbrellas and lounge chairs, creating a sense of comfort.

The exotic marine life and endless snorkeling opportunities are a paradise for any nature lover. As the day ends, the beauty of the majestic mountains and the breathtaking sunsets, with vibrant orange, pink, and purple hues reflecting off the calm sea, adds a delightful bonus to a Caribbean adventure.

In 2007, I had the privilege of exploring the adventure and excitement in Jamaica. Everything I had envisioned came true, but nothing prepared me for the stark contrast between the warm hospitality indoors and the annoyance of the persistently approaching vendors outdoors. It was like stepping into a serene, cozy room, only to be abruptly pulled back outside into the discomfort of the intense heat and suffocating humidity. The contrast was so intense, it was like experiencing two different worlds in one place.

Vendors waved trinkets and souvenirs with persuasive smiles, begging tourists to buy or look at their handmade jewelry and local crafts. The persistent pressure, like a relentless heat, made it difficult to enjoy the surroundings.

Sometimes, there was little to no respect for the tourists. For example, while walking next to your significant other, the guys would hit on the ladies instead of selling merchandise, even if the couple were holding hands. But, if you keep walking and ignore them, there are no confrontations.

So, visiting Jamacia can be a bit of a nuisance, but it's an excellent place for a vacation.

That same year, 2007, I introduced my son to his first cruise adventure, opening the door to a world of discovery and joy. As an enthusiastic traveler, I wanted to share my passion for exploring new places with my children, hoping to fill their hearts with unforgettable memories. My daughter was of age and decided not to go with us. So, my son and one of his best friends, whom I consider my second son, accompanied us on the journey instead.

Carnival Cruise – Western Caribbean

As we stepped aboard the Carnival Cruise Lines ship bounded for the Western Caribbean, the boys' eyes widened with wonder. They marveled at everything, from the sparkling pools to the busy dining halls. They pile their plates high with food, just as I did on my first cruise. One would think we hadn't eaten in days!

The boys enthusiastically jumped into the pool, their excitement mirrored in their wide, beaming grins. They engaged in a spirited race down the water slides, their laughter filling the air.

After a quick dry-off, they headed to the arcade, challenging everyone to beat their high scores on the video games. In the evening, they eagerly joined the kids' club playing more games and preparing for the nightly dance party. My son, who is not particularly fond of parties, still participated with his best friend, a testament to their strong bond and his willingness to adapt.

As a parent, I maintained a low profile, observing their every move on the ship. They relished every moment, from the never-ending pizza at the buffet to the thrilling treasure hunts on the deck. Each day brought a new adventure, and their anticipation for what's next was palpable. Watching them take it all in, their youthful curiosity sparking with every discovery, filled me with immense pride and joy while feeling *mission accomplished!*

Honolulu, Hawaii

In 2015, I had the privilege of visiting Hawaii, a dream come true. It was a journey of a lifetime, exploring the stunning islands of Honolulu, Maui, Kauai, and Oahu with my best friend and her family.

Our visit to Honolulu was exceptional, as we made a trip to Waikiki Beach and had the unexpected delight of seeing the cast of the *Hawaii Five-O* series from 2010 to 2020. As a devoted fan of the original series, which aired from 1968 to 1980 and starred Jack Lord as Steve McGarrett, I was initially skeptical about the new series, which starred Alex O'Loughlin as McGarrett and Scott Caan as Danno. However, as I immersed myself in the show, my skepticism gradually diminished and I began appreciating the reboot.

The view of the beach was fantastic, with families spreading colorful blankets and umbrellas over every inch of the sand, leaving no room to sit or even stand. Children dashed between sunbathers, kicking up sand, while some built complicated castles. The scent of sunscreen and saltwater filled the air while seagulls hovered above, eyeing the countless picnic baskets.

Despite the lack of space, the vibrant energy of the crowd created a lively, fun, and sun-soaked atmosphere. And then there was the

Hollywood magic added by the cast of *Hawaii Five-O* that made that particular day more electrifying and enchanting. The atmosphere was electric, with some lucky fans even speaking with the cast. I was able to take a few photos as I looked on in amazement.

Kauai, Hawaii

Affectionately known as the Garden Isle, Kauai offers personal discovery and adventure. Its breathtaking, lush landscapes and vibrant botanical gardens provide a treasure trove to explore.

When I stepped onto its shores, the island's natural beauty immediately seized my heart. Hearing so much about the gardens in Kauai was overwhelming, and I couldn't wait to explore them.

The entrance of the National Tropical Botanical Garden, a place of serene beauty, etched itself into my memory. It was a paradise of lavish greenery, vibrant blooms, and the rich scent of tropical flowers. The gentle rustle of leaves added to the enchantment.

Exotic plants from all corners of the globe thrive in this unique environment, displaying the incredible variety of tropical flora. The palm trees, swaying gently with the breeze, cast patterns of light and shadow on the ground, creating a peaceful atmosphere. The journey was a personal haven as I leisurely strolled through the garden's meticulously crafted pathways, feeling a sense of peace and calm.

The McBryde Garden, too, was a symphony of colors and textures, serving as a sanctuary for native Hawaiian plants. Rare orchids and bromeliads cling to tree trunks, their bright petals splashing color against the green canvas. The garden is alive with the soft hum of bees and the occasional butterflies, creating a dynamic, living portrait of nature at its finest. I am constantly amazed and in awe of God's sense of color, beauty, and creativity, with countless wonders to admire.

Our next adventure in Kauai transformed the scenes that had once flickered on my TV screen into vivid reality. A lei gently rested on my neck and a Mai Tai—a delightful blend of rum, orange curaçao, fresh lime juice, and almond syrup—tingled on my taste buds. I felt a deep, personal connection to the island's spirit.

It was my first luau, a celebration of Hawaiian culture and traditions: the rhythmic beat of the drums, the mouthwatering scent of roasted pig and tropical flowers, and the dancers in their grass skirts whispering with each graceful sway all spoke to me in a language uniquely Hawaiian. The luau was a masterpiece of sights, sounds, and scents, each contributing to the overall experience.

The meticulously carved designs on wood transformed into stunning works of art and crafts: bowls, masks, and sculptures that highlighted the wood's natural grains and textures, capturing the essence of Hawaii's natural beauty and storied past. Overall, it was a magical experience that left me in awe of the beauty of Hawaiian culture and traditions.

Then, I came across the blowhole, a rare geological wonder where water surges into the air through lava tubes beneath Hawaii's rugged coastlines. This unique and awe-inspiring sight completely captivated me, filling my eyes with wonder and my heart with awe.

Like an excited child, I dashed to the edge of the viewing area, my laughter echoing with each spectacular burst of water. My camera, a mere tool at that moment, fought desperately to capture the sheer beauty of the scene, frustratingly failing to do justice to the magnificence before me. It was a battle between my excitement and the task, a struggle that only added to the moment's grandeur.

After leaving the site, I captured stunning photos of jagged cliffs rising from the ocean and intricate rock patterns and formations, adding to my lasting experiences and memories.

Maui, Hawaii

As we soared above the islands of Hawaii, particularly Maui, a breathtaking landscape that embodies the essence of paradise was unveiled. The experience was made even more intriguing by the unique Mokulele Airlines aircraft, with its single propeller engine and cozy nine seats. Gliding over the Pacific's sapphire waves, this unique vantage point highlighted the dramatic contrast between the deep blue ocean and the islands' lush greenery.

As we neared Maui, its rugged coastline, adorned with beautiful beaches, was a remarkable sight. The sun's rays reflected off the water, creating a shimmering path that directed our gaze to the lively reefs below, a testament to the fearsome natural beauty of this island paradise.

Our visit to the Iao Valley State Monument, a place of natural dignity and profound cultural heritage, was an enlightening journey into the heart of Maui. The monument, home to the towering 2,250-foot-high Iao Needle, also known as the phallic stone of Kanaloa, the Hawaiian god of stone, is a striking symbol of the island's wartime history. It was significant for ancient Hawaiian warriors, who admired the needle as a symbol of strength and protection.

As we entered the valley, we were greeted by generous greenery that created a cocoon of nature. The tranquility deepened as we ventured further, accompanied by the sight and sound of cascading waterfalls, babbling brooks, and the whispers of the Iao Stream's winds. Its clear water reflected the vibrant foliage.

Our exploration along the well-maintained trails introduced us to a rich variety of native plants and flowers, a testament to the island's biodiversity. The numerous informational plaques provided detailed insights into the valley's historical and cultural importance, connecting ancient traditions that shaped the land. It was fascinating to learn that the sacred site of the Iao Valley was once a royal burial ground for Hawaiian chiefs.

Finally, as the plane circled back to the main island, the sight of the sun setting over the Pacific Ocean painted the sky in brilliant shades of orange, pink, and purple. The islands below had a golden glow and beauty amplified by the fading light. This aerial journey over Maui and the surrounding Hawaiian Islands left a compelling impression, a reminder of the fantastic beauty within this tropical paradise.

As I departed from Maui, the island's beauty lingered in my mind, leaving a lasting impression unlike any other place I have visited. Every corner of Maui offered a unique blend of natural splendor and cultural richness that captured my heart. Without a doubt, Maui stands as the most beautiful island I have ever had the privilege to explore.

Oahu, Hawaii

Lastly, we visited the Pearl Harbor historic sites in Oahu, delving into the profound history and touching memories of that fateful day.

As we explored the memorials and exhibits, we felt a deep connection to the past and a renewed appreciation for the sacrifices made. We then explored the USS *Bowfin* submarine, a living testament to World War II history, docked at Pearl Harbor. Instantly, we transported ourselves back to the 1940s, envisioning the lives of the brave sailors who once called this vessel home. The narrow passageways and compact quarters underscored the submarine's functionality, designed for resourcefulness and efficiency during wartime missions.

Navigating these tight spaces, we felt like children in a playground, moving slowly due to the confined quarters. We were captivated by the dials, levers, and periscopes that once steered the submarine through the treacherous waters. But it was the tour guides' stories that truly brought the experience to life, amusing us with gripping tales of *Bowfin*'s numerous successful patrols and daring activities in the Pacific theater. We could almost hear the echoes of commands and feel the tension that gripped the crew during those pivotal moments of battle.

Moving on to the torpedo room, we were amazed by the massive torpedoes stacked neatly along the walls. The precision and care required to oversee these powerful weapons became apparent as we listened to stories of *Bowfin*'s impressive combat record. Each compartment we visited revealed more about the daily lives of the sailors, from their sleeping quarters with tightly packed bunks to the mess hall where they shared meals and brotherhood.

Our journey on the USS *Bowfin* concluded on the deck, where we took a moment to reflect on the submarine's legacy and the courage of its crew. Standing under the Hawaiian sun, we gazed across the harbor, feeling a profound sense of gratitude for the sacrifices made by these silent warriors. The experience gave us a deeper understanding of the submarine's pivotal role in history and a lasting admiration for the men who served aboard it.

Visiting the USS *Arizona* Memorial was also a profoundly moving experience. As we approached the white, floating structure by boat, the site's significance began to sink in as a potent reminder of the lives lost during the attack on Pearl Harbor on December 7, 1941.

The atmosphere was silent, filled with admiration from visitors who were quietly reflecting on the history beneath the still waters. The simplicity of its design immediately struck us. The open-air structure allowed the gentle Hawaiian breeze to pass, creating a peaceful ambiance. We walked along the marble walls, each inscribed with the names of the 1,177 sailors and Marines who perished aboard the *Arizona*. Each name represents a story, a life cut tragically short, and the collective loss weighed heavily on all visiting the site.

Looking over the edge, we could see parts of the battleship still visible beneath the water's surface. The oil droplets, often referred to as the "tears of *Arizona*," slowly rose to the surface, a heartbreaking reminder of the ongoing legacy of that day. We stood in silence, watching these dazzling drops break the surface, each symbolizing a life and a moment in history that continues to resonate.

Inside the shrine room at the far end of the memorial, a wall of names stood as a powerful tribute to those who gave their lives. The room's solemnity is palpable, and the weight of history is almost tangible.

As we left the memorial, we felt a deep respect and gratitude for the sacrifices and a renewed commitment to remember and honor the legacy of the USS *Arizona* and its crew. The visit left an indelible mark on us, a profound reminder of the cost of peace and the enduring importance of remembering the past, a duty we now carry with us.

Orlando, Florida

In 2016, I had the privilege of visiting the Holy Land in Orlando, Florida, a journey that engaged me in biblical history and culture. The replicas of ancient Jerusalem's gates were a sight, transporting me to a different era. The stunning replica of the Western Wall, a place of prayer and reverence, is a model of Jerusalem during the Second Temple period, providing a comprehensive view of the city's layout, complete with sophisticated details of temples, palaces, and lively streets.

However, it was the Scriptorium that genuinely caught my curiosity. This ancient manuscripts and artifacts treasure trove holds a unique story within each piece. One artifact that particularly intrigued me was a portion of the Dead Sea Scrolls, a significant find that shed light on the religious practices of the time. As I examined the stories behind each artifact, I was captivated by their preservation and significance in shaping religious traditions, a testament to the enduring power of faith.

The most captivating part of my visit was the grand reenactment of Jesus Christ's life at Calvary's Garden Tomb. The dramatic portrayal, featuring live actors and captivating special effects, vividly brought to life the events of Jesus' crucifixion, burial, and resurrection. This was not just a moving experience, but also an enlightening one, as it deepened my understanding of the spiritual essence of the Holy Land. The experience was educational and deeply meaningful, fostering a connection to the timeless stories and teachings that continue to inspire millions worldwide.

San Diego, California

When my son landed a job as a game designer in San Diego, California, in 2016, it was a perfect opportunity to visit him and see the city, so I added it to my bucket list and off we went for a weekend visit.

My BFF, my son's godmother, and I enjoyed our travel adventures together. We spent most of our time at the flea market, where we indulged in local crafts and tested-tasting authentic street food. We also explored the Old Town Museum near our hotel, which took us back in time with its well-preserved artifacts and immersive exhibits while my son was at work.

Stepping into the Old Town Museum was like stepping back in time, a nostalgic journey to the city's early days. The detailed exhibits brought the past to life. We explored the blacksmith shop and watched live demonstrations. In the bustling marketplace, we had a unique experience of browsing handcrafted goods while savoring the market revolution of nineteenth-century commerce.

While trying different restaurants, we soon learned that we preferred Tex-Mex over authentic Mexican food, probably because that's what we were used to eating.

The Old Town Museum vividly captures the essence of San Diego's rich heritage, making history tangible and engaging. We enjoyed the visit, but once was enough. It's not a place I feel drawn to revisit.

In contrast, despite the unpleasant odor, La Jolla Beach offered an unforgettable experience, with seals and sea lions basking in the sun. Their unique sounds—a symphony of barks, snorts, and groans, each with its own distinct tone and rhythm—almost overpowered the smell, blending harmoniously with the rhythmic crash of the waves.

In her own world, BFF was not captivated by the scene. The overpowering stench was all she could focus on, and she was ready to leave. But for me, observing seals, a species known for their playful nature, basking lazily on the rocks, their contentment evident as they stretched out and soaked up the warmth, was a fantastic sight. I had never witnessed their behavior, and it added a touch of untamed beauty to the coastline.

I stood there, captivated by the soothing rhythm of the waves crashing against the shore, completely absorbed in the coastal magnificence before me. My deep, unwavering love for nature and the seals' habitat drives me to look forward to revisiting their famous resting place.

Dominican Republic

In 2018, I enjoyed a unique vacation at the Luxury Bahia Principe Esmeralda in Punta Cana. The resort's prime location, offering the best beaches and world-class dining, was further enhanced by the exceptional service. Every moment felt catered, as if the staff knew exactly what I needed to make my stay special.

The late-night beach entertainment was a highlight, with one of the most amazing shows featuring a Michael Jackson look-alike, an electrifying performance complete with his dazzling costumes and precise choreography. It was my favorite!

The Dominican Republic, a haven of luxury and excitement, extended its thrill beyond the resort. It gave me a gateway to several heart-pounding excursions: a buggy ride, a zipline, horse riding, and a safari. Despite my initial hesitation, I quickly realized that these adrenaline-fueled adventures also offered a unique perspective, enlightening me about the grand landscapes and exciting culture of the Dominican Republic in a truly inspiring way.

As someone who's not particularly fond of getting dirty, especially during adventurous activities like buggy rides, the mix of anticipation and apprehension on my face was palpable as I approached the buggies. I carefully climbed into the vehicle, avoiding any spots with mud or dust— "nice nasty," as my beloved grandmother used to say. Her words of wisdom, a constant companion, echoed in my mind, shaping my every move as I kept my hands tucked close to my body and my eyes fixed ahead, ready to dodge any potential splashes or dirt.

When we hit a muddy patch, I couldn't help but let out a squeal and lift my feet off the floor with a mix of discomfort and determination. Despite the rough and messy ground, I managed to maintain my composure, and my desire to stay clean was a constant challenge that kept me engaged in every careful movement. The surge of excitement and anticipation was undeniable. The adrenaline was building as the engine roared to life, and we sped off into the scenic landscape.

Next on my list was ziplining, and the anticipation was intense as I geared up and approached the tall platforms. Being my first time, I was excited and nervous, so my BFF and I decided to zipline together. The guides expertly secured our harnesses, and we launched ourselves into the air with a deep breath. My BFF rode in front, and I held on behind her for dear life. I remember her shouting, "Let go of me!" which only made me grip tighter.

But as I found myself midway through the ride, a surprising sense of calm washed over me, a peaceful pause in the midst of the thrill. At that point, I felt the thrill of soaring above the treetops, looking down from what seemed like several hundred feet above the ground while staring into the distant hills. After this exhilarating experience, a moment of pure adrenaline, I was prepared for my next adventure, horse riding.

Years ago, I ventured into horse riding, a sport familiar to me through my son's involvement in the Boy Scouts. As I mounted my horse, the initial nervousness was quickly replaced by excitement as I ventured onto the trail. The sound of gravel crunching under the horse's hooves, the gentle sway of the horse's body, and the sight of the peaceful green forests all merged, creating a humbling, tranquil setting. This setting made me feel a close and peaceful connection with nature, bringing a deep sense of serenity and preparing me for the next adventure, the safari.

The safari tour was more than just an adventure; it was a captivating educational journey and the perfect way to conclude my excursions. Excited to explore the diverse wildlife and landscapes of the region, I boarded the open-air vehicle. Our guide, a true expert in his field, not only enriched our experience but also reassured us with his profound knowledge of the local ecosystem. We were fortunate to spot everything from exotic birds to playful monkeys.

The most exhilarating part of the trip, and a highlight I can't forget, was milking a cow—an exciting and educational first-time experience. The safari offered a rich experience, allowing me to

Life Realities

deeply appreciate the natural wonders of Punta Cana in a way I had never imagined.

Cape Cod, Massachusetts

Martha's Vineyard, the uniquely charming island south of Cape Cod, had always been on my bucket list. In 2022, I finally embarked on an exhilarating journey with the H-Town Travelers from Houston to Cape Cod, Massachusetts, to experience its magic firsthand.

The anticipation of the trip was palpable, and the island's appeal is undisputable, with its gorgeous historic New England homes offering a window into the region's rich and fascinating heritage. Many of these homes are now museums, like the Atwood House Museum in Chatham, where you can explore the past through old-fashioned furnishings, artifacts, and exhibits.

The island's charm truly came to life as I strolled through the streets, soaking in the history and beauty around every corner. For anyone who loves history, this enchanting destination is necessary on their bucket list.

Cape Cod, Massachusetts, exhibits many museums, such as the Sandwich Glass Museum, the JFK Museum, the Korean Memorial, and the Zion Union Heritage Museum, which offer fascinating insights into its rich history and culture. I was blessed to visit all four of them.

145

I found the Sandwich Glass Museum to be an absolute must-visit, especially if you're fascinated by the art and craft of glassmaking. Located in the charming town of Sandwich, the museum displays an extensive collection of stunning glassworks, including sophisticated blown glass pieces and historic glass objects. Watching the live glassblowing demonstrations was a highlight, as I learned about this delicate art form's complex techniques and rich history.

The firsthand exhibits, which encourage active participation, made my visit not just engaging, but also highly educational. The museum's colorful displays and interactive experiences truly offer something for everyone, captivating visitors of all ages.

In Hyannis, the John F. Kennedy Hyannis Museum is a unique tribute to America's 35th president. Positioned in the heart of the Kennedy family's beloved summer retreat, the museum is a rich origin of photographs, personal artifacts, and multimedia exhibits that trace JFK's life, presidency, and his enduring connection to Cape Cod. Stepping into the museum, you'll be immersed in the profound bond between the Kennedys and this scenic region. The museum's thought-provoking displays present a distinctive perspective on JFK's impact on the nation and his cherished moments on the Cape, making it a must-visit for history enthusiasts and tourists alike.

Meanwhile, just a short distance away, The Cape Cod Korean War Memorial in Barnstable is a significant tribute to the brave men and women who served during the Korean War. This touching memorial features a striking bronze statue of a soldier surrounded by plaques bearing the names of local veterans. The calm and peaceful setting, amidst the breathtaking beauty of Cape Cod, provides a place for reflection and remembrance, honoring the sacrifices made by those who fought in the "Forgotten War." Visiting the Korean War Memorial is a powerful reminder of the courage and dedication of Cape Cod's service members.

Equally crucial in its tribute to local history, the Zion Union Heritage Museum in Hyannis celebrates the region's rich cultural heritage and the priceless contributions of African Americans and Cape Verdeans, significantly shaping Cape Cod's history. This vibrant museum, with its rich tapestry of diverse exhibits, including historical artifacts, art, and collectibles, is a testament to its profound impact on the area's culture. These exhibits are more than just a collection of items, they are a journey of resilience, creativity, and achievement stories that enlighten and inform visitors.

The Zion Union Heritage Museum is a vital cultural resource, nurturing greater understanding and appreciation of the area's diverse heritage. Each museum offers a unique and enriching experience, providing visitors with a more profound knowledge of Cape Cod's multifaceted history and culture. Whether you're marveling at the artistry of glassmaking, delving into the legacy of JFK, honoring war heroes, or celebrating cultural diversity, Cape Cod's museums promise to leave an impression on every traveler, stimulating their intellect and broadening their perspectives.

Of course, I must mention the windmills, lighthouses, and my favorite, the cranberry bog, a breathtaking must-see attraction in Massachusetts. The Eastham Windmill, the oldest on the Cape, has been meticulously restored and stands proudly as a symbol of the town's agricultural heritage. In Brewster, the Harris-Black House and Higgins Farm Windmill, part of the Cape Cod Museum of Natural History, offer a unique educational experience. Here, you can learn about the milling process and the vital role these structures played in the local economy. Their rustic beauty provides a unique insight into Cape Cod's agricultural past, making it a must-visit for history enthusiasts and tourists alike.

Similarly, the Highland Light in Truro, Cape Cod's oldest and tallest lighthouse, is not just a beacon of beauty but also a significant part of the region's cultural heritage. Climbing to the top offers not just breathtaking views of the Atlantic Ocean, but also a journey through time.

The Nauset Light in Eastham, with its distinctive red and white stripes, is an amazing sight, offering scenic views and a fascinating glimpse into the life of a lighthouse keeper. These historic lighthouses, with their unique charm, not only provide spectacular photo opportunities but also serve as beautiful reminders of the Cape's rich maritime history.

Lastly, seeing the most beautiful mauve or dark pink flowers covering a bed of water instantly sparked my interest. The tourist guide explained that it was a cranberry bog. Like a famous oil painting, it was stunning, almost deceiving my eyes, especially since I had yet to learn how cranberries are grown.

I was fascinated, and couldn't understand why I had never learned about the unique process of growing cranberries in school. I couldn't wait to start researching and find out more about it. *HowStuffWorks* gave me the first insight into such a fantastic, thought-provoking concept. It reads: "plants that grow in bogs must contend with a host of unfavorable conditions, but the cranberry plant's durability allows it to survive in this habitat" (Avery, 2023).

For example, cranberries need fresh water to survive. Of course, the fact that bogs consist of mostly acidic water represents a challenge to the plant. Luckily, the fruit's woody stems are tough, and their small leaves have a leather-like consistency. This enables the plant to retain as much fresh water as possible by restricting the amount of usable water that passes through (source: Johnson). The plant's fine roots also absorb and use organic nitrogen to survive, despite the scarcity of nutrients in the bog's sterile soil (source: Eck).

Moreover, cranberry vines are resilient—an undamaged one can last indefinitely. Some vines in the cranberry bogs of Massachusetts are more than 150 years old (source: CCCGA) (Avery, 1970).

Its unique landscape's natural beauty and agricultural substance are incredible! I cannot emphasize enough how seeing acres of cranberry bogs in full bloom is a mesmerizing experience.

Antigua and Barbuda, Again

The thrill of returning to Antigua for the second time with a different group of friends was obvious. I was eager to explore familiar spots, but this time, I was determined to create unique experiences and memories that would last a lifetime.

To achieve this, we planned a diverse range of excursions, each offering a unique thrill and adventure, from sailing and cruising until sunset to ski boating and ziplining—activities I didn't get to try on my first trip to Antigua.

Our first adventure, sailing on the beaches of Antigua at around 6:30 PM, was perfectly timed to enjoy the beauty of the Caribbean waters. The scenery was a breathtaking display of oranges, pinks, and purples that danced across the visually stunning Caribbean waters, creating an unforgettable, impressive scene.

As I set sail from the perfect shores, the white sandy beaches and rich green hills provided a stunning backdrop, a sight that inspired amazement and made me feel like I was gliding through a postcard. The waves gently lapped against the boat, the salty smell of the sea filled the air, and the warm breeze caressed my skin, making the experience a complete sensory journey.

Along the way, I encountered secluded coves and hidden bays only accessible by boat; their natural beauty added to the fascination of the journey.

The next day, the moment I'd been eagerly anticipating arrived—it was ski boating time! I climbed into the ski boat with the help of the owner and driver. I felt the sun's warmth on my back and the scent of sunscreen surrounding me as the boat's engine roared to life and we plunged into the cool, refreshing water.

It was a liberating experience as the wind played with my braids, the water danced on my face, and the powerful hum of the engine, drowning out all other sounds, added to the thrill of riding a ski boat for the first time. As we navigated through the waves, the splashes of water on my face and the rush of adrenaline were invigorating. I felt a sense of freedom and life, a symbol of the trust between the driver and me. I was in good hands, and that trust kept me engaged and liberated throughout the ride.

The sun's final rays vanished below the horizon and the night sky exploded with a dazzling array of stars. Filled with gratitude, blessings, and excitement, I ended the day and drifted into a peaceful night's sleep.

Our final excursion was a thrilling dive into ziplining and aerial adventures. While ziplining in Antigua was enjoyable, it didn't match the thrill of the Dominican Republic.

In Antigua, I zipped through the air on 11 or 12 short lines for 2 to 3 hours, but it felt closer to the ground, and the scenery didn't excite me much. The Dominican Republic offered a longer, more exhilarating ride, making the Antigua experience feel like a letdown in comparison. It left me craving a more thrilling adventure.

Since I'm not one of those adrenaline addicts like the contestants on *Survivor* who get stranded in isolated locations and rely on their survival skills, the aerial adventures exhausted and terrified me. My heart raced as I climbed higher and higher, gripping the ropes with sweaty palms. Each step felt like a battle against my fear of losing balance on a tightrope.

I could feel the people's frustration behind me, wondering what took me so long to move forward. Every obstacle was challenging and nerve-racking, so I begged one of the workers to walk towards me and meet me midway. I didn't think I could make it. Heck, I didn't want to make it!

But then, something changed. I pushed through the fear and as I reached the end, I felt relief and empowerment. My legs were shaky, and my mind was shutting down from that one endurance attitude, but I had overcome my fear towards the end, which was a powerful feeling. Nevertheless, it was an experience I want to avoid repeating.

Boulder City, NV – Hoover Dam

Just when I thought my 2024 vacations had come to a close, I was pleasantly surprised with an irresistible invitation to visit the Hoover Dam—a landmark on my bucket list since my teenage years. The journey was extraordinary, with the breathtaking beauty of the ancient rock formations along the way to Boulder City serving as custodians, leaving me amazed at their timeless watch over such a desert landscape.

As we approached this manufacturing sight, the sheer scale of the Hoover Dam took our breath away. Standing before its enormous structure, we were genuinely impressed by its awe-inspiring engineering brilliance.

The dam rises like a gigantic concrete monument, its curved walls sweeping gracefully across the canyon, seamlessly integrating with the natural landscape. The elaborate art designs etched into its surfaces, a testament to human creativity, add a touch of elegance that is truly admirable. From the top, the dam's massive form plunges downward, holding back the deep blue waters of Lake Mead on one side as sunlight glints off the concrete while the Colorado River winds through the rugged canyon below. The dam's smooth lines and magnificent presence symbolize the mastery of human craftsmanship, creating a powerful contrast against the surrounding red rock landscape. These lines convey its strength and purpose, guiding the eye along its graceful curve. More than just a structure, the Hoover Dam is a testament to human ingenuity and respect for nature's power, a fact that fills me with a deep sense of admiration.

I am so grateful and sincerely appreciative of those who allowed me to experience the Hoover Dam firsthand. I will cherish the pictures and memories for a lifetime.

There are many adventures left to explore and add to my bucket list as I move forward. As I check each one from the list, I feel a rush of satisfaction and excitement. Each new journey is a delightful surprise, making me feel alive and eager to see what incredible adventure awaits me next.

The joy of discovering new destinations, their unique cultures, and breathtaking landscapes is a feeling like no other. The thrill of completing one vacation blends into the anticipation of the next, making every moment a celebration of life's endless possibilities.

I'm already brimming with anticipation, eagerly awaiting the next incredible adventure that life has in store for me. As I embark on the next chapter of my journey, I can't wait to explore the following destinations from my current bucket list: Africa, Aruba, Belize, Budapest, Cabo Sa Lucas, Canada, China, Dubu, Switzerland, Thailand, and The Grand Canyon.

As I eagerly look forward to the future, I'm confident that I'll uncover even more thrilling places. Each destination will spark new adventures, expand my horizons, and fill me with awe for the world's endless wonders. With every journey, I'll dive into the unknown, driven by curiosity and excitement, and most importantly, eager to embrace the unexpected. The future is full of untold possibilities, and I'm prepared to seize each one, knowing that the road ahead promises unforgettable experiences and stories waiting for me to unfold.

SPECIAL THANKS TO MY READERS

Thank you from the bottom of my heart for taking the time to read *Life Realities*. Your support means more than words can express, and I hope the lessons and reflections within this book not only resonate with you but also enrich your personal journey.

As you reflect on these lessons, I hope they inspire you to take action. Your journey, along with the journeys of those who shared their stories, is a unique and powerful one. May these stories ignite a spark in you to step out, embrace your next chapter, and explore the magnificent world our Creator has given us to enjoy. These lessons have the power to transform, to open new doors, and to lead you to a brighter future. As you venture forward, may you find new perspectives, deeper connections, and the courage to pursue all life has in store for you!

i

---

[i] https://www.gotquestions.org/Bible-intuition.html

www.ingramcontent.com/pod-product-compliance
Lightning Source LLC
Chambersburg PA
CBHW072012090426
42740CB00011B/2160